Into the Paradox

Conservative Spirit, Feminist Politics

D1715383

Toni A.H. McNaron

ISBN: 978-0-9895341-2-3

Library of Congress Control Number: 2013942760

Published by Hurley Publishing
Minneapolis, MN

To my mother,
who introduced me to God.

For John
with all good wishes:
fondly)
(Torri

Table of Contents

Introduction

When I tell people I spend Sunday mornings at a Roman Catholic church, I am usually met with some combination of amazement and dismay: "How can you, a clear-eyed, radical lesbian feminist, possibly choose to belong to such a misogynistic, homophobic, and corrupt institution?" When I've shared my intention to write this spiritual memoir, several of these same people have told me that I have an obligation to speak about the tight-rope I walk so that I can get something precious and crucial to my life in the present and into the future. Here is that explanation.

This tracing of my spiritual path surely makes clear that church-going has been part of my life from a very early age. What seemed at one point a compulsory rejection of the Episcopal church for its inability to serve the world around it left me spiritually bereft, even though my walking out still seems an act of integrity in light of my belief that faith must grapple with politics. Once I sobered up after nineteen years of isolated and miserable drinking, I came gradually to register just how lonely my soul felt not to have a physical space to which to repair periodically in order to hear familiar words of worship. In such a setting, I could hope to renew my sense of being part of a community. Ironically, it was within the framework of Alcoholics Anonymous (AA) that I found my way back to "God," though not to the images of that force or idea that had been given to me as a child and young person. Every time I said the phrase in Step 3—"God as we understood God"—I inched my way closer to being able to walk into a building devoted to Christian ideas and ideals. AA provided me with what would come to be the lifeline I needed to return to organized religion: "Take what you like and leave the rest." I believe I am strengthened in ways not entirely clear to me by staying within a faith community which also tolerates and even promotes people whose views on certain issues offend me. If I want my society to embrace me in my various degrees of "otherness," then surely I need to be willing to see beyond or around bones of contention that might let me consign members of that society the same pariah status. I see this conclusion as a paradox and not a contradiction.

On a more nuanced level, why have I returned to Christianity rather than embracing another faith system such as Buddhism which has many appealing aspects? Or why not Hinduism that ascribes meaning and value to all of creation, not just to us humans? Or why not Judaism that certainly affirms ritual, and that celebrates prophets as prescient as Isiah? Perhaps the answer to these questions lies in the simple fact that I weep every Palm Sunday, as the gospel is read about the initial exaltation of Jesus of Nazareth, followed breathtakingly fast by his trial and crucifixion. Clearly, this particular story gives me a context in which to unite spiritual belief with worldly politics. I think of instances that have occurred during my own lifetime in which we have behaved similarly, lauding a given politician or community leader only to reject him or her when their behavior hasn't conformed to some theoretical standard of acceptability. And I let myself identify with how betrayed and confused Jesus may have felt between the moment Judas kisses him to signal his enemies as to his identity and his final acceptance of his crucifixion as part of God's plan for him and us. So I will continue to worship as a Christian. And, when I receive the wafer during the Eucharist each week, I will reconnect with my profound sense of the huge generosity of Jesus, who let himself be executed so painfully in order to fulfill his sense of what God intended for him as his final act as a human being.

Finally, I wrestle with the question of why I have chosen to become a Roman Catholic rather than making eventual peace with my once-beloved Episcopal Church. To have returned to St. Mark's Episcopal, only half a mile down the avenue from the Basilica, would have meant I would have to ignore repeated betrayals over many decades by individual ministers to whom I looked for spiritual guidance. To embrace the spiritual and liturgical world within which the Basilica exists, I have to ignore some policies and pronouncements of the institution of the Catholic hierarchy focused in Rome. Actually, I don't think of myself as going to "a" or "the" Catholic church. I go to my parish where my spiritual longings are nourished. The Basilica is one of a handful of liberal congregations in Minneapolis, and its staff somehow manages the doctrinal minefields thrown up by the Pope and our ultra-conservative diocesan Archbishop in order to serve the diverse community that comes through its doors. Their ability to do that makes this particular church a place where I can deepen my own relationship with Jesus and God. So my decision to remain a member in the face of official positions and pronouncements that infuriate and sadden me is finally personal and entirely local. I could never belong to a more conservative parish, so I feel tremendously blessed to have found the Basilica.

———

As I inhabit my seventies when more telephone calls and e-mails tell of illness, loss of loved ones, and deaths, mortality presses in upon my consciousness and I find myself pondering end-of-life and afterwards. My living will makes crystal clear that I do not want any extraordinary measures used to keep me breathing. "Life," to me, means far more than the intake and exhalation of breath, even though I am moved by the idea that at my creation, a force beyond my comprehension invested me with the "breath of life." Instructions to my dear friend and executor are equally adamantine: "If they take me to a hospital in some 'emergency,' get me out of there and back into my home as quickly as possible. And pay whatever it takes to keep me there until I die."

Of course, my hope is to die quickly, not to linger with some progressive illness such as cancer, most assuredly not to descend into the fogs of dementia. But I have no control over how (fast) I exit this world, so often I turn my thoughts to whatever it is I believe happens next. Though every Sunday I say that I believe in "the resurrection of the dead and life everlasting," that does not call up images of some place called heaven. And, since I understand how metaphors work, when I hear about our bones being knit up into some post-earthly version of ourselves, I just convert that to the idea that, once I have moved beyond the frets and strains of this life, my spirit will be at peace, hence "whole" again after the fragmentations that inevitably "break" us.

When I face the question of immortality, as so often happens in my life, literature comes to my aid. There is a passage spoken by Jim Burden, the deeply flawed narrator in Willa Cather's classic, *My Antonia*, in which he is attempting to explain how he felt on the occasion in his boyhood when he "was entirely happy." He says: "Perhaps we feel like that when we die and become part of something entire, whether it is sun and air, or goodness and knowledge. At any rate, this is happiness; to be *dissolved* [italics mine] into something complete and great. When it comes to one, it comes as naturally as sleep." Jim is remembering the moment when he first met Antonia while he is in an Edenic garden setting, resting in the sun against a large pumpkin, looking at the world around him. In the earthly world, I find this sense of dissolving or losing my "busy" self in the glorious music sung by the choir at my church. Indeed, my prayer after lighting my three-day candle each week is that I can make myself open to what occurs during the service so that I can experience this crucial loss of ego, this stilling of all the wheels usually spinning in my brain.

Since this dissolution of the busy self is my highest goal while alive, it follows that my ideas of immortality would be similar. So at times, as I am brushing my teeth or setting out the recycle materials, I indulge in the fantasy of "What happens to 'me' when I stop breathing? Do I go to some other realm or do I just dissolve into calcium deposits?" On a walk recently, a friend asked me what I thought about life after death and I said mostly I didn't think about it, that I agreed with Milton that we make our own heavens or hells right here on earth. After a pause, however, I went on to say that I actually knew where I wanted to "go" when I stopped breathing— into Edmund Spenser's Garden of Adonis. By 1596 Spenser had completed half of a very long poem he planned to write. Entitled *The Faerie Queene*, its purpose was to set forth the twelve virtues required to become a gentleman within the framework of Christian humanism so popular during his lifetime. In Book III of the six projected books he managed to execute, he broke with custom and had the model of the virtue be portrayed by a female. Britomart is the hero of this book devoted to the central virtue of Chastity. Because this concept has changed significantly since Spenser's day, a 16th century definition is called for here. Originally, the word chastity meant "true to one's innermost self," and could exist in humans who were no longer technically virgins, be they men or women. Britomart is shown in armor, as an Amazonian figure who combines salient masculine qualities with feminine beauty. She teaches King Arthur the true nature of chastity so that he can eventually assume his place as the ideal ruler.

Venus figures centrally as this story unfolds, and in Canto VI, she conducts her "babe," Amoretta (little loved one) to what Spenser calls "her joyous Paradise/Where most she wonnes [dwells], when she on earth does dwel" (Stanza 29). This Edenic spot is the famous Garden of Adonis, the place where Venus entertained the beautiful young man she wanted as her lover. One corner of it is where I imagine my soul will be once I no longer exist in human form. I choose this locale because of its physical and spiritual qualities, offered here in Spenser's own wonderful words. Early in the description, he says the Garden is "the first seminarie/Of all things, that are borne to live and die,/According to their kindes." I like to imagine dwelling where all "the goodly flowers" began. At the entrance to the Garden, an old porter called Genius regulates traffic into and out of this idyllic place. His job involves sending out each "babe" to her or his earthly home and then readmitting those who are blessed to return to their origins. Once readmitted, this is what Spenser says:

> After that they againe returned beene,
> They in that Gardin planted be againe,
> And grow afresh, as they had never seene
> Fleshly corruption, nor mortall paine.
> Some thousand yeares so doen they there remaine;
> And then of him are clad with other hew,

Or sent into the chaungefull world againe,
Till thither they returns, where first they grew:
So like a wheele around they runne from old to new.

(stanza 33)

This vision of renewal of life forms suits my current ideas of immortality, so I am content with the story I tell myself about my eventual life in a mythical garden. The fact that I envision eternity in a garden also coincides with the deep connections I make between gardening and being in touch with God.

So I will continue parking under the freeway across from the Basilica of St. Mary, walking into the narthex where I dip my left fingers into the holy water before entering the church proper. I'll light my three-day candle into which I put those I love who may be experiencing hard patches, and I'll pray for the openness needed to help me surrender to what may happen in the Eucharistic service. I will then spend an hour or so repeating words of comfort and power being spoken and heard around the globe. So I will become part of a vast "congregation" of individuals trying to connect their small individual existences to something larger and grander than they. I will work hard to approach the God I have come to accept with the sense of wonder essential to comprehending that which will always remain ineffable.

Preface

$\mathcal{I}$ began writing this faith journey the morning after Pentecost Sunday, 2009. For those who do not observe a liturgical year, Pentecost is a major event in the Roman Catholic calendar. At my church, it's also the last Sunday our ninety person choir sings until early September, so the music that day is special. We have triumphant trumpets and trombones with robust tympani accompaniment. A "bell tree," which is the familiar name for the fifteen small brass bells, mounted in rows on a wooden standard, precedes the choir as it enters and exits the sanctuary, their carrier shaking them vigorously to produce amazing sounds. Lots of congregants, including me, wear red because Pentecost is the day we mark the tongues of fire descending upon the twelve disciples and Mary, the mother of Jesus, ten days after Christ is taken away in or by a cloud, after having made several reassuring appearances after his earthly death. The Acts of the Apostles speaks of those tiny fiery missiles as the Holy Spirit descending to remind unsure and frightened followers of God's love so recently expressed through an incarnation into the man, Jesus. The words say that as the tongues landed on individuals, each began to speak in a different voice, but that all could understand. As I ruminated on the meaning of this seeming paradox that Sunday morning, I flashed to earlier descriptions of the Tower of Babel, where many languages are spoken and no one can understand anyone else, producing verbal chaos. What made the multiple voices different this time?

Then I remembered moments at operas when the four principals just stand still on stage, facing the audience, and sing, all at once. I'm personally particularly fond of these quartets in Puccini's *Turandot*. I remember when I was new to opera, I'd try hard to decipher what each "voice" was saying, to no avail. Eventually, I learned that I was to step back, harmonically, and listen to the total effect of the merging sounds. From that perspective, I could hear and comprehend the meta-narrative unfolding in sound. What was the overarching emotion the four singers were trying to convey? Once I stopped using intellect to "figure it out," I was washed over by the sheer force of the blended voices. And I "knew" what the moment was trying to "say." So it must have been for those present as the "cloven tongues as of fire" (The Acts, 2.2) landed on each of their heads, inspiring them to speak from their spirits rather than their intellects.

Usually moved by the Pentecostal service, something was different on this occasion in 2009. I think it may have been the combination of my musings during the sermon about how many languages could be simultaneously understood and the recessional hymn, entitled "Fire of Flame, Undying Fire," (words by Albert Bayly). The opening lines brought me to complete attention: "Fire of God, undying flame,/Spirit who in splendor came,/Let your heat my soul refine,/Till it glows with love divine." The simple mysticism embedded in this idea of God excited me intellectually, since metaphysical poetry has long been a favorite form for me. My love of 17th century poetry and prose led me to write a dissertation on John Donne's sermons and to teach Shakespeare for the entire thirty-seven years of my academic career at the University of Minnesota.

I left church in tears as the big bronze bells in the high bell tower rang out the end of worship. As I drove my car out of the parking lot, I remember being accosted by my car radio as I turned on the ignition. I needed to leave Garrison Keillor's "A Prairie Home

Companion" for another day. I wanted to listen to the echoes from the great bells as I drove up the avenue toward home.

The bells at the Basilica are quite special, given by someone who wanted them to symbolize the depth of their own faith. Forged at the Royal Eijsbouts foundry in the Netherlands, there are six of them of varying sizes and tonalities. I have learned that the process of forging a great bell is exacting and time-consuming, involving the making of a "false" bell that serves as the mold for the final pouring of bronze. To lower tonality, slivers of the bronze are carefully shaved off from the interior, and a mistake in this tedious procedure can mean abandoning the bell entirely and starting all over again. Finally, it is the clapper that determines what sound the bell will make once installed. It seems custom dictates naming such sacred bells and those at the Basilica carry the names of New World saints: Elizabeth Ann Seton (American, 1774-1821), Juan Diego (Mexican, 1474-1548), Katharine Drexel (American, 1858-1955), Kateri Tekawitha (Native American, 1656-1680), Andre Bessette (Haitian, 1845-1937), and Pierre Toussaint (African American, 1766-1853). My heart always leaps when, on a clear, non-humid day, I hear these same bells as I garden in my front yard, over a mile away from the Basilica.

As the resonant sounds of our six bells were fading that Pentecost morning, I heard myself say, aloud to no one, "I want to write about faith." Unnerved by this uncommon outburst, I wondered where it had come from, later dismissing it as a passing fancy that would not last through a good night's sleep. I didn't have a good night's sleep, however, and found myself next morning at my computer screen, opening a new file called "faith journey" and beginning to write. So began what has come to be this book, a place where I have tried to shape language about something ineffable, to "forge" my own sounds about my relationship with God.

My first challenge was in the diction itself, since "faith" can have diverse connotative meanings in our culture. For me, the word is separate from, though may exist within, organized religious practices. I have known people with profound faith in reason or science or astrology or even capitalism. My understanding of the term "faith," however, is not in reference to a belief "in" something but rather to a state of being in which I am able to hold fast to the unseen or ineffable aspect of existence. It is certainly true that I depend upon certain tangible practices to assist me in achieving and maintaining this irrational state, so much that follows here will focus on where and under what conditions my faith has been nourished and bolstered as well as questioned and blunted. At this point in my life, the Roman Catholic religion contains more of those practices than I can find in any other formal setting. But the "journey" traced here involves multiple venues and resources.

I have a story to tell about what I am calling my faith journey. As a seventy-six-year-old, white woman, I find myself, on Sundays, seated in a pew at a huge Roman Catholic church in Minneapolis. How I came to be there and why I stay there puzzles and amazes me if I think about it. Certainly I find the Catholic church's official stance on several issues close to my heart unacceptable. To keep refusing to ordain women as priests, even as parishes languish because there are not enough men going into seminaries to staff ministerial openings, makes no sense even as it flies in the face of my decades-long engagement in feminism and the empowerment of women. To join others in protesting a woman and her family's right to terminate a pregnancy early in the process confirms the church hierarchy's lack of respect for women's right to choose how to live our lives. And, to continue issuing encyclicals condemning same-sex relationships and to urge governments to pass constitutional amendments denying marriage equality to lesbian and gay couples tells me that, at some abstract level, I, as a lesbian, am not welcome by all at the altar railing.

In my pew, however, I feel completely at home. Next to me most Sundays sits a lovely, thoughtful white man whose wife is in charge of liturgy at another parish where the music is contemporary, so her partner worships at the Basilica. Next to him some days sits a retired priest and former student of mine, also white, with whom I now have tea on a regular basis so that we can talk about things spiritual and liturgical. Behind me most weeks is a sweet, white, heterosexual couple who seem genuinely pleased to see me and to exchange the sign of peace with me. In a section to my right sits an older heterosexual African American couple whom I've known as colleagues at work for decades. Near by sits the white lesbian visual artist who worked for fifteen years as artist-in-residence at the Basilica, giving us powerful images on the covers of weekly worship leaflets and periodic epical decorations of the vaulted space above us. She is a specific casualty of papal bigotry, having been put on permanent suspension because she spoke out against the church's stand on gay marriage. She continues to attend, having told a local reporter who asked her if she would leave the church because of its anti-lesbian/gay stance, "Certainly not, I'm as Catholic as the Pope." Like her, and with her as a model, I will not let what's wrong with Roman Catholicism at the institutional level override all that is "right" about it for me.

Knowing full well that my present is inextricably entwined with my past, I begin this memoir with my earliest recollections of time spent in a church. That place is a tiny shingle building in Fairfield, a suburb of Birmingham, Alabama. It was not a Roman Catholic parish but rather an Episcopal one, tiny because the South of my childhood was dominated by the Baptist church. The formation of my ideas about a belief system comes, then, from a denominational source with a long history of trying to find a *via media* or "middle way." This approach comes from a recognition of genuine diversity of opinions on something as complex as faith in an unseen God.

But my Episcopal heritage also failed me on several important occasions, leaving me in my sixties with strong reliance on God, but with no spiritual home where I could go on Sundays and be part of something larger than myself. For entirely extra-religious reasons, I began attending the Basilica of St. Mary in Minneapolis: my life-partner sang alto in its large and accomplished choir, so I went on occasion because she wanted me to hear a piece, often in Latin, that they were going to sing. When that same life-partner told me in the fall of 2006 that she wanted to end our relationship, I sought refuge in that giant edifice with its stunning rose windows and massive pipe organ and liberal priest. My attendance has gone from about once a month to every week, and the liberal priest has retired from the Basilica so that he might better serve the multi-racial parish just north of the church. But being in that congregation continues to connect me to something mysterious and powerful that I choose to call God.

———

When I first set out to write this "faith journey," I thought only to recount a series of memories and vignettes of my life in and out of the church. As draft followed draft, however, patterns emerged and the story unfolding became much more complex and tangled. Once I began reading portions aloud to friends and, later, asking several people to critique what I had written, it became clear that I either had to define the project narrowly as personal therapeutic writing or go deeper into anatomizing my current ideas of God, Jesus, faith, and worship. I believed I had done that when I finally sent a draft to a friend who is also a rigorous reader/critic. When I heard her say that I still had not explained clearly to skeptical readers just what is crucial to my faith and to my observances of it, my heart sank. "I really don't want to do this," I argued weakly.

In the days since that conversation, I've thought and prayed about my heavy reluctance to do what I know will enrich this spiritual memoir both for me and for many readers. A metaphor that catches my feelings exactly comes from the gardening world. As a passionate gardener whose front yard does not contain a single blade of grass, I have on many occasions decided to plant bulbs in the fall so as to have early blooming things in the Minnesota spring. Jonquils, tulips, and hyacinths have gone into the cooling earth in November, only to put forth lots of green leaves and virtually no blooms in April. The reason for this is simple: I ignore instructions that say to bury the bulbs a full eight inches in the ground. After I've dug and dug, my old wooden ruler still only measures five or six inches. After asking myself "what difference would a couple more inches make," I drop bulbs into the ground and cover them up, full of hope for what will appear the next spring. Reason tells me I am not digging deep enough to allow the bulbs to mature fully and produce flowers, yet I stop an inch or so short.

Over and over in my life, I have pulled myself back from those extra two or three inches because I haven't wanted to learn or feel what I know exists in that remaining space. What that might be in the case of my spiritual journey seems clear if elusive: If I find myself weeping during one special musical offering at church, I don't play more music upon getting home because to extend or prolong the emotions that come up might mean I would have to alter some fundamental aspect of my life. When the gospels speak of Jesus' gathering his original male disciples, he usually has but one short sentence to them: "Put down your nets (or other tools that define them at that moment) and follow me." The disciples are said to have obeyed immediately, without pondering consequences or possibilities. I'd like to imagine I could have done that in their place, but my reluctance to go to the core of my beliefs or to the essence of what I need to express my faith suggests that I'd have asked for a few days to consider Jesus' offer. And that delay would most likely mean I'd find a way of declining it. So the challenge to me at this point in my life is to stop pulling back, to simply plunge into the deeper spaces of my spirit.

If I can do that, go down to find the essence of my faith, then this project may resemble the beautiful tulip or hyacinth I look for each spring but hardly ever see because I've refused to dig the final inch. To keep at such a spiritual "dig," I must believe that new and powerful knowledge lies buried deeper than any first, second, or even third drafts can reveal.

Chapter 1
Early Exposures

*A*s a child of six or seven, during the 1940s, I often found myself on Saturdays at that tiny Episcopal Church in my home town, where my mother was a mainstay. Baptists dominated the white Southern religious landscape, with Presbyterians and Methodists coming in a distant second As a religious minority, perhaps Southern Episcopalians reacted by coming to see themselves as at least one cut above the other Christians in their midst. While this religious elitism flourished, what appealed to me, even as a young person, was playing under pews and in the big sandbox that was part of my Sunday school experience. Christ's Church, as my church was named, held about fifty people and was kept in fine condition by the women's auxiliary composed of five ladies from the congregation. When Mamie, the name most people and I used for my mother, went there on Saturday afternoons, it was to arrange flowers for the altar, and polish all the brass appointments. She also slid the correct little square cards that told worshippers what hymns to find in their dark blue hymnals into tracks in the wooden board tacked to the wall at the front of church. Her last act was to place over the stiff board that covered the silver chalice those linens she had so recently washed and ironed. Though my family employed a wonderful African American woman, Josephine, to do housework that included washing and ironing, Mamie took on the church linen herself. When, once I asked her why she didn't have Josephine help her, she replied, lamely, "Well, Honey, this is my way of serving the church—and Josephine might scorch the linen or let the iron tear through the lace border." Even as a child, I knew how unlikely it was that Josephine would injure anything she ironed, since she applied that hot and heavy object with absolute care as I watched her in our basement. About once a month, we drove down to church early on Saturday morning so Mamie could get on her knees, not to pray (though perhaps she did that while she worked), but to wax the floors and pews. Under those seats, I often amused myself, crawling around as I imagined advancing on the Axis armies. I knew about those forces because my father, who sometimes put a small comb below his nose, flattened his gray crew cut, and imitated Hitler, told me often and at length all about their marches and attacks.

Our church had a small, old-fashioned pump organ, and sometimes my mother would take a break from cleaning to play it. If I happened to be scurrying around on the floor, I could feel the deep vibrations from the base chords that got louder if Mamie moved her feet faster on the two big pedals that sent air into the system to produce sound. While she played, I usually lay very still as those thunderings coursed through my body. Once, after I'd been taking piano lessons for a while, when I was about ten, Mamie let me play a few notes on that organ, but my legs weren't long enough to allow me to pump hard so as to make "big" sounds while simultaneously hitting the right keys on the keyboard.

By the time I was eight or nine, I was helping polish the brass appointments: a large and heavy cross with IHS etched into its center; two seven-branch candelabra that were a real challenge to get clean because candle wax stained them green every week; a small, lighter-weight cross mounted on a wooden pole that was carried in front of the choir and rector as they entered and exited each Sunday; variously sized vases in which the weekly flowers were arranged. There was also silver to polish at least once a month: the chalice with its plain cup but very ornate stem that required a toothbrush and much scrubbing to get shiny enough to please my mother; the paten that held the communion wafers and was easy to clean because it was utterly flat and unadorned; and a tiny set of communion objects—cup that held one sip of wine, pill box for the wafer—used when our minister paid a house call to someone too ill to make it to the altar rail. I liked the miniature cup and dish because they were quite like my tea sets at home that I used to entertain myself and my imaginary friend who, unlike my parents, was always available to join me. These days, I polish silver once a month, though it's personal and secular pieces, inherited from my mother, and cherished by me. The fact that I insist on using Wright's silver cream, when ads promise easier and better results from "newer" products, ties me back to my youth, when occasionally Mamie let me help with the holy silver if I were extremely careful and precise.

Caring for these sacred things taught me to view the church with the same attention I was learning to have for the antique ornaments at home. Mamie must have seen her role as someone to keep beauty, secular and religious, in tact, and she passed this along to me. It didn't seem strange that I spent most Saturdays in a quiet church instead of playing with other children on my block, any more than it seemed unusual to go, after Sunday services, to Elmwood Cemetery to "tend" the graves of Mamie's mother and father. My grandmother had died three years before I was born and my only memory of my grandfather, who died before I was three, is of his holding my hand while we walked down our front sidewalk. Because he refused to bend his ever-straight back, my memory is of having to strain my own arm in order to keep hold of his putatively supportive hand. Whenever I read the name and dates on his marker, I wished he'd lived long enough to let me know something about him that wasn't filtered through my older sister's lens in which he was without flaw. Because I never even saw my maternal grandmother, I measured her character only through my mother's devotion to her.

What we did those Sundays in that quiet outdoor space at Elmwood, surrounded by granite markers and occasional wrought-iron benches, was weed, water, plant annuals every spring, and replace wilted flowers with sprightly new ones in the sunken metal cylinders that served as receptacles at the head of each grave. We also took picnic lunches of cold fried chicken, mayonnaise sandwiches, and generously sweetened iced tea to enjoy on a bench we commandeered from a lot near our own. These days I watch a lot of video tapes of my favorite "Mystery" detectives. One of those is Inspector Morse, a lonely, gruff, opera-loving, beer-drinking, crossword puzzle-working sleuth who is vulnerable to any woman remotely kind to him. In one of his cases, that woman works in her parish church, where he comes upon her one day. She says she is "garnishing" the church and Morse is hooked, since he also adores words, especially arcane ones. If I think about it now, that is precisely what my mother did all those years at Christ Church and at our cemetery lot.

Church, then, in my childhood, was really about my mother and me. My father attended Christmas and Easter services only, preferring to spend the other fifty mornings sitting in his bathrobe in his wicker rocker in the back bedroom. He read the expanded Sunday "funnies" or the latest issue of *The Saturday Evening Post* or *Bluebook*, a popular monthly story magazine published by the same company that eventually published *McCall's*, a monthly glossy geared expressly to women's interests. I never heard him speak about God or Jesus or Christianity, though during a phase when I wanted to know my parents' favorite psalms, Daddy told me his was # 1. One of the shorter of David's offerings, this psalm speaks about those who do and do not "walketh in the counsel" of the godly, with clear emphasis on what will happen to those who do not do so: they are "like the chaff which the wind driveth away"; they "shall not stand in the congregation of the righteous"; their ways "shall perish." Lots of judgment here and very little of the protection and care present in many other psalms. So, did my father pick this one on the spot, just to enter into my little survey, choosing #1 precisely because it was first and so may have held his attention at some point? Or did he actually know what it said, and, if so, did he then feel more like the ungodly or the godly? (By the way, my mother's favorite psalm was # 91, while mine, at that point, was # 121, both of which proclaim the expansive and sustaining protection of the Lord's love.)

My sixteen years' older sister, Betty, is mostly absent from my early religious experiences since she was either away from home or insistent on shutting the door of her bedroom on Sunday mornings so that she could sleep later after one of the countless "dates" with one of her several swains. When I asked for her favorite psalm, she shrugged and talked about the latest serious work of literature she was reading by William Faulkner or Henry James or Marcel Proust, as if these were her source of wisdom and reality. Betty occasionally was cajoled or guilted into going to church with Mamie and me, usually wearing a huge hat that kept anyone sitting behind her from seeing the minister as he stood at the altar. She never sang the hymns, having been told by someone early in her own childhood that she "couldn't carry a note," and believing it.

I was fine with Daddy's and Betty's not attending church, since it meant I had some part of my mother's life mostly to myself, apart from the other two grown-ups in the house who seemed often to draw her away. So going to church came to be connected with being close to my mother in a literal sense, even as she also helped me grow spiritually by talking with me about what she believed. The only other time Mamie seemed to "belong" to me was when I stayed home from grade and junior high school, "sick" but still able to follow her around the house in the afternoons as she dusted or cooked. By the age of about nine, I knew how to hold a thermometer against my teeth so it would rise beyond the normal designation, because if I had a "fever," I got to stay home. Report cards show more days absent than days present and include comments on the back like "How smart Toni seems to be, but couldn't she come to school more often?" When I stayed home, I learned far more than when I went off to the sub-standard school rooms where tired teachers had lowered expectations to such a degree that I was bored most of the time. But Mamie taught me math and English, talked about wonderfully advanced stories like *Treasure Island* and *Little Women*. She furthered my secular education just as she was nurturing my spiritual development on Saturday afternoons and Sunday mornings.

———

Growing up Episcopalian meant I seldom heard about hell or evil or punishment, the cornerstones of Southern Protestantism. Instead I participated in a Sunday school that involved coloring pictures of Jesus performing miracles or suffering the little children to come unto him. For years, that verb, "suffer," didn't make sense to me, since the sheets of paper we got showing Jesus with people like me were full of smiling faces and kind words, whereas I knew that "suffer" meant quite the opposite because my mother, already in her late forties, often complained of unspecified aches and pains both in her body and her heart. When we handed in our finished coloring of a scene from the life of Jesus, our teacher stuck a little sticker on our foreheads. There were three different bird stickers in her box—a brownish bird, probably a thrush; a bright red male cardinal; and a beautiful deep blue bird. Though she never said anything to anyone who got the drab bird, we all knew the "best" bird was the blue one for some unstated but absolutely certain reason. I never got a thrush but usually had to settle for a cardinal stuck in the center of my forehead or pasted onto my picture as I rejoined my mother in the chancel. Blue birds went mostly to little girls who colored within the lines and told the teacher how much they liked hearing about Jesus.

In addition to coloring, we occasionally sang simplistic songs like "Jesus Loves Me." Singing wasn't much fun for me since my grade school music teacher, who came to our room once a week and taught us strange songs like "On the Road to Mandalay," kept telling me I was singing notes too low for a girl, suggesting that neither of Mamie's children could "carry a tune" musically. After these little sing-alongs and about fifteen minutes before we were returned to the grown-ups, our teacher would lift off the sheet of plywood we'd been coloring on, revealing what was my favorite part of the morning's regimen—a massive sandbox that lay hidden under the plank. We were free to play as we chose. Objects in that sandbox had nothing to do with Jesus or church or prayer. There were little metal trucks of all colors, lots of animals of various sizes and species, and tiny shovels and buckets. I liked to invent long trips full of hazards for my little truck or to make animals out of wet sand. Whatever the reasoning behind this aspect of the program, it suggested to me that Sunday church could be fun, just as crawling around on the floor on Saturdays was fun.

Years later as I have listened to the vestigial agonies and angers of friends and partners who grew up in strict Protestant or even evangelical denominations, I have often cast back to my magical sandbox under the wooden table top and been grateful because my earliest idea of God spared me the rules and severity that seemed to come with too much of American Christianity. These days, as I happily drive off on Sunday mornings to the Basilica of St. Mary, some of that childhood ethos returns. The music we sing is often about dancing and shouting joyfully to God, behaviors strictly forbidden to my Baptist neighbor children. The Bible is seen as a text full of stories framed by Jesus and the various prophets and disciples to show us mere mortals how to act better in our daily lives, not as absolute truths by which to judge and condemn those around us while hobbling ourselves from participating in life's pleasures. "Holiness" at the Basilica feels more like moving little trucks through the sand or finally getting a blue bird (instead of that red cardinal because I colored outside the lines) pasted on my forehead than it does following dictates from some stern "god" with a frown on his face and the prospect of eternal damnation in his pronouncements. Of course, there are difficult demands placed on anyone trying to emulate Jesus' ability to love broadly; loving one's neighbor is not always easy if that neighbor has turned up his or her loud music at one o'clock in the morning, or if their cat kills lovely nuthatches who have thought of your own yard as a sanctuary with seed and shade. But I am able to work to be a better person when I allow sensory beauty to sustain me, and I strive for a way to place love and acceptance at the very center of my being.

The Basilica calls itself a "big tent church," code these days for "lesbians and gays and people of color are welcome." Certainly there is ample literal room for the full spectrum of humanity; the building itself is a mammoth structure, built at the turn of the twentieth century by imported Italian artisans and with imported marble. So there is a touch of comic irony when the priest uses the euphemistic phrase in one of his homilies. The approach of my parish runs counter to official decrees and doctrines coming down from the Vatican. This means, of course, that I have to ignore most of the official positions taken by the papacy and its more conservative representatives. I have a model for doing this that comes from almost forty years in AA and other twelve-step groups. There, we are told to "take what you like and leave the rest," said in order to help an amazingly diverse population of strongly opinionated individuals remain members of their recovery communities. What I like at church is the music, the rituals of the liturgical year, the sense of being part of a large group of people, all of whom are engaged in the same spiritual practice, and the certainty that resides in the fact that the same words are said every week (except for the sermon and special petitions).

Chapter 2
Growing in My Faith

*T*he journey between the sandbox days and my present worship at the Basilica of St. Mary has often been punctuated by a sense of how my concept of God or Jesus didn't conform to what my culture told me were prescribed definitions. To me, as a young person, God was an old white, bearded man who was extremely powerful, able to divide the sea into two halves in order to help his favorites in a battle. But God was also someone who made all the animals and plants, the flowers my mother loved to put into her beds and then bring into our house when they bloomed. Jesus, though also white, was young and healthy, able to walk long distances and climb tall mountains from which he preached. He also loved little children and was often depicted surrounded by people very like me. Neither God nor Jesus was ever presented to me at home or in Sunday school as judgmental or mean-spirited, so I just thought of them as invisible beings who magically knew and cared about me.

An early instance, however, in which my ideas and ways of worshiping clearly set me apart from my peers occurred when I was about ten. On my block I had two playmates, sisters in a devoutly

Baptist family. Their father, Mr. Rivers, carried his dog-eared Bible around with him both inside and outside his house; I never recall seeing him without its being open to some key passage, which he often and quickly took time to read and begin to explicate to me before I found some way to slip from his ideological clutches. The two daughters, Agnes and Sarah, went to church a lot, it seemed to me. Sundays, of course, but for much more of the day than I ever did. And then they couldn't play outside with me because their parents believed that they, like God, must "rest" on the seventh day. Sarah and Agnes also went to church on Wednesday nights, to something called a prayer meeting, which I eventually learned was precisely that, a meeting where people prayed for themselves and other people. In summers, my buddies spent several weeks just outside of town at Vacation Bible School. The summer I was ten, Sarah asked me if I'd like to attend one of the week-long schools and I said yes. Mamie wasn't keen on the idea because she feared I'd somehow contract impetigo or stay in the sun too long and burn myself. Finally she agreed, since the camp only lasted from ten in the morning until about two in the afternoon, and there were lots of adults there to watch out for us. I remember, however, her brief but pointed words to me before I went off the first day: "Now, Honey, remember that the people you'll be with today believe different things than we do at Christ Church, but they are good people, and I dearly love Annabel (my friends' mother) who is a kind and good person."

Monday about nine in the morning, Mr. Rivers put down his Bible long enough to drive the three of us to their church where a big truck was waiting to take us to the camp. I'd never ridden in a truck bed, so the adventure began on a glorious note. As we happily rode through Fairfield and into the country, we belted out "It's the B-I-B-L-E,/Yes that's the book for me/ I'll stand alone on the word of God/ The B-I-B-L-E!!!" Many people on the streets waved at us and smiled broadly, clearly approving of our song and our project.

Once at the campsite, I was immediately struck by all the huge pictures on the walls of the little wooden building where we were to learn. All of them were of Jesus, some surrounded by children, many showing him on top of a tall mountain with lots of people spread out way below him. He conformed to the conventional image—tall and young with long blond hair and extremely white skin. One that disturbed me a lot was of Jesus looking angrier than in any of the coloring pages I'd been given. He was tossing people out of a big church. Not only was the image unfriendly, but the caption underneath seemed too stern for "my" Jesus: "SINNERS PUNISHED" was not a phrase I'd heard from my minister or Sunday school teacher. Since I didn't know the story about the money-lenders, I had no way of understanding that I was to feel good about what Jesus was doing. So I puzzled over this aspect of a man I associated with smiles and love.

The only activity I can remember our engaging in was plaiting a bracelet. This was a popular activity during my childhood, on the level with macramé during the 1960s, or tie-dyed shirts in the 1970s, or legos and perle beads more recently. Each of us was given several long strands of what I believe must have been highly polished plastic. We were then shown briefly how to entwine four of these to make tiny square lengths that were eventually tied off by our instructor. Then we could wear these around our wrists. My squares were not "right," because some of the little units were fatter than others, so there was no uniformity to my bracelets. The finished product looked more like a pregnant caterpillar than a piece of jewelry. We were also supposed to make two of these items, one for ourselves and one for our mothers, but because my first try had those lumps, I was excused from making a second one. My friend Sarah perfectly executed her bracelet to take home to her mother, while I was told to watch her and try to see how to do it better the next day. This exclusionary move reminded me of the disturbing picture on the camp room's wall of people being cast out of church. It also fit in with my having a "too low voice" for a girl, and coloring outside the lines.

I also remember lunch that Monday at Vacation Bible School. It was peanut butter and jelly sandwiches that must have been made in Fairfield very early that morning because by noon when we sat down to eat at a long wooden table outside, the bread had dried badly and the peanut butter was runny from the heat. We had something to drink with these leathery and gooey sandwiches that I'd never before even seen—Kool-Aid. My usual summer drink was homemade lemonade that even included a slightly beaten egg white because my mother was sure that would make my blond tresses shine. The Kool-Aid was a shade of pink that hurt my eyes and, because there was no refrigerator at this camp, and it was a hot summer day, the beverage had gotten quite a bit above room temperature. The final touch was more successful—Oreo cookies that couldn't get "worse" for standing in their packages from early in the morning. Before we could have any of this questionable fare, however, there was a blessing. At home, we said a blessing before dinner, though not before mid-day lunch, especially if it were a picnic. That blessing was short and clear in its import: "God is great, God is good, so we thank Him for this food. Amen." Baptists must not have deemed this serious enough because a man who was clearly a minister stood before us and prayed for what seemed a very long time. We were to remember that there were little children in other places, particularly in Africa, who were starving and didn't "know the Lord." Since nobody I knew talked about "knowing Jesus," I was confused about how that made far-away children any different from me. The minister also told us to pray for the sick, for old people, and for sinners. I remember trying to pay attention to what he was saying, but I was hungry and didn't know yet about how dry and oozy my sandwich was going to be. So I secretly prayed that each pause would be the end, and we could have our lunch.

The ride back into Fairfield was as much fun as it had been earlier that morning. The song we sang once inside the city limits was one I didn't know, so I mostly listened: "This little light of mine, I'm gonna let it shine" was easy to learn, though there were several verses and I couldn't keep up, what with the swaying and bumping in the truck bed. Sarah's mother, Annabel, was waiting in the church parking lot, so we piled into their dark green Dodge sedan. She didn't ask us anything about Vacation Bible School, which surprised me, since every day when I got home from regular school Mamie sat me down and invited me to rehearse what I'd learned in each subject. I recall deciding that Sarah's mother would wait until they were inside their own home before inquiring about what the day had held. Then she'd be so pleased to get that perfectly plaited bracelet.

Once at their house, Sarah took me aside and asked a question that will never fade from my memory: "Have you been baptized, Toni?" "No," I said in all innocence, "we don't do baptism, but I was christened when I was a little baby and I'll take confirmation classes when I'm eleven so I can be confirmed into the church when I'm twelve." Then Sarah looked at me quite seriously for one ten-year old to another and said: "Well, then, you know if you die before you're twelve, you'll go to hell." Even though Episcopalians didn't talk about hell, I knew it was a place no one wanted to be, so I ran up the hill to my house, burst inside, and, before Mamie could ask me what I'd learned that day, I blurted out: "Am I going to hell? Sarah says I am because I haven't been truly baptized."

Obviously Mamie had known more than she let on when she made her seemingly bland comment as I was leaving that morning. Not only did Baptists believe different things from us, they clearly thought they had some superior system for living and dying. My mother hugged me hard and replied, "Honey, of course you're not going to hell. You were christened—remember the little long, white dress I have in the trunk in Daddy's and my bedroom? And once a baby is christened, Jesus loves you and God loves you and you'll go right to heaven whenever you die. Now don't you worry any more about this." She let me go and went into the kitchen to make me a big glass of VERY cold, VERY good iced tea. While drinking my tea, I had pulled out my bumpy first try at plaiting and told her, tearfully, that it was all wrong, so I wasn't allowed to try to make one for her, and I was sorry. She got the same expression on her face as when I asked her if I were destined for hell, a look that signaled that she would defend me from all comers and that what they had said and done was unacceptable by her lights. By the time I'd drunk my glass of tea, my mother had obviously come to a firm decision: "You are not going back to that school tomorrow. We'll go to the 10-cent store instead and I'll buy you some plaiting strands, and we'll practice until you make a beautiful bracelet."

True to her word, we went to Kress's the next day, and I got to pick out four wonderful shades of plait: royal blue, egg-yolk yellow, forest green, and fire-engine red. As if by magic, Mamie knew just how to pull each strand in tight before looping the next one, so my next attempts yielded much better results. Soon I was making really spiffy bracelets—three for me, one for her, one for my sister, and one for my father who never wore it. When I told Sarah I wouldn't be going out to the camp, she seemed genuinely disappointed. She also never brought up hell again, so we kept playing together. A few years ago, I found out her current address from a former neighbor with whom I correspond occasionally. I wrote Sarah, she wrote back, we seemed pleased to be back in touch. I eventually came out to her as the lesbian I've been for decades, and she never responded. December holiday letters came for a year or two, but after that there has been no word. I continued sending my card until just this past year when it seemed disrespectful to myself to continue down what had become a distinctly one-way street. I can only hope that Sarah does not now think she was absolutely right back when we were ten, except that she now has a surer reason for my "going to hell" than my not having been properly baptized as an infant.

———

Confirmation classes, undertaken when I was eleven, didn't deepen my beliefs because most of the time was spent memorizing answers to questions we would be asked by the bishop at the ceremony. But they lasted many months during which I decided to think on my own about what it was I was repeating. While no official encouraged me to do this, my mother had insisted for years before that moment that I tell her what I thought about myths and even nursery rhymes. At one point in the Offices of Instruction, people preparing to be confirmed are asked: "What do you mean by this word Sacrament?" The reply held a particular fascination for me: "I mean by this word Sacrament an outward and visible sign of an inward and spiritual grace given unto us; ordained by Christ himself, as a means whereby we receive this grace, and a pledge to assure us thereof." The Offices of Instruction spend a lot of space trying to clarify just what this opaque answer might mean. For instance, the questioner asks "What is the outward part or sign of the Lord's Supper?" to which we were to reply "The outward part or sign of the Lord's Supper is Bread and Wine which the Lord hath commanded to be received." The process continues "What is the inward part, or thing signified?" with my answer being, "The inward part, or thing signified, is the Body and Blood of Christ, which are spiritually taken and received by the faithful in the Lord's Supper."

Long before confirmation, I had accepted that all statements were not literal. When read to, I often believed the stories, only to have my mother allay my distress or fear or sheer puzzlement by saying "Oh, Honey, that didn't really happen; it's a story and so things stand for other things." Metaphor was part of my grasp of the world, so I fully understood that the tasteless little wafer people ate on the first Sunday of each month (our parish was, like most in the South at that time, distinctly "low" church, which meant only two candles and a few flowers on the altar, and Communion only once a month) stood for Christ's human body. I fully accepted, on that level, the fact that his body was sacrificed so that we Christians could somehow know God's love. It was not that body itself, since to believe that would just be silly. Jesus had died almost two thousand years before I would soon begin kneeling at the altar rail to have a wafer put into my outstretched hands. By my early twenties, I thought that people who believed in transubstantiation were actually creating tiny false gods by believing that they were somehow eating Jesus—either that or they were bordering on some weird spiritual cannibalism. It seemed much more powerful to see myself about to reenact what went on in that Upper Room when Christ first gave bread and wine to his disciples. At that time, his disciples probably did not think that the bread "was" Christ's body or that the cup of wine "was" his blood. He was seated at table with them, fully substantial, like his fellows. And his instructions to repeat this action carried a clear symbolic message, i.e. "Do this in remembrance of me." Recently, a former Catholic priest and liturgist showed me a passage from Sermon 272 by St. Augustine in which Augustine is explaining about the nature of the sacraments received by the congregants. "St. Paul tells the faithful: *Now you are the body of Christ, and individually you are members of it* [italics mine]. If that is so, it is the sacrament of yourselves that is placed on the Lord's altar, and it is the sacrament of yourselves that you receive." Amazingly modern and radical, this description makes perfect sense to me.

The confirmation ceremony itself was not performed at my home church. Rather twelve-year olds from all over the city converged on the Church of the Advent in the middle of downtown Birmingham. That was where the Bishop presided, and it was the Bishop who would lay his hands on our heads and confirm us into the church so that we could receive Communion. That church was as ornate as my Christ Church was spartan. The high altar, reached by traveling down a very long nave, was marble with baroque decorations on its front: the left panel showed a thin cross behind an equally thin lamb, while the right panel was a crown of thorns. The key central panel depicted a *bas relief* of a dove that seemed about to take flight with its elaborate olive branch held firmly in its beak. The organ in this church was not a foot-pumped contraption but rather a gigantic console with four banks of keys and endless pipes of varying lengths. I was sure no child would have been allowed to crawl amongst this church's pews while his or her mother tended to altar appointments. Being in this space was a formal occasion, where going to Christ Church with my mother had been an activity full of playfulness and warmth.

The Episcopal bishop of Alabama in 1949 was the Right Reverend C.C.J. Carpenter, and no one seemed to know what those three initials stood for. He was massive and imposing. Well over six feet, his shock of snow white hair and bushy eyebrows made him seem like one of the giants in my childhood story books. Completing this heroic aura was his voice—a sonorous *basso profundo* that easily filled the space of that huge building, even in the days before priests became "miked." Clad in deep purple robes, wearing his pointed miter and carrying his sterling silver crosier, he strode down the aisle as the organ played reverberating chords that I felt in the soles of my feet newly shod in black patent leather Mary Janes and thin white socks. All of us who were being confirmed were sitting together in the front pews with parents seated in a reserved section behind us. (I no longer can remember if my father accompanied Mamie for this special service; my older sister was not present.) The boys wore suit jackets, white shirts, and dark blue ties. They all looked distinctly uncomfortable in this formal attire. We girls wore white dresses with no adornments allowed, not even a little black ribbon. Bishop Carpenter delivered the opening prayers in the Order of Confirmation and then asked us to stand as a group and respond in the affirmative to the key question, "Do you promise to follow Jesus Christ as your Lord and Savior?" Another short prayer followed in which he said words I would later parse with serious concentration: "daily increase in them [us] thy manifold gifts of grace: the spirit of wisdom and understanding, the spirit of counsel and ghostly strength, the spirit of knowledge and true godliness; and fill them, O Lord, with the spirit of thy holy fear, now and for ever."

I remember catching my breath when the Bishop said "holy

fear," since what I knew about fear didn't fit with everything else he was hoping would "increase" in us now that we were entering more fully into a relationship with the Lord. I was so afraid of the dark that I wouldn't go from my bedroom across the dining room into the kitchen to get a glass of water in the night. There was nothing "holy" about that. When I asked Mamie what that phrase meant, she was evasive, saying something like "Well, all things are different if they pertain to God or Christ." Theologians have written often and in varied ways about this concept, but the idea that seems most helpful to me is this: The fear of God is a holy awe or reverence for God's injunctions and instructions. In any event, as I knelt waiting my "turn" with the Bishop, I concentrated on the other promises he was offering to me if I lived as Jesus expected me to. I would know, however, what "holy fear" might feel like years later as I stood behind Niagra Falls where I was sure God resided.

What happened next is something I can still enter into if I fall to my knees and close my eyes. Bishop Carpenter asked us to come to the altar rail and kneel before he began making his stately way from person to person. Onto each bowed head, he put his hands: "Defend, O Lord, this thy Child with thy heavenly grace; that he/she may continue thine for ever; and daily increase in thy Holy Spirit more and more, until he/she come into thy everlasting kingdom. Amen." When he approached me and repeated those lines just for me, I felt suddenly important to God, in a heightened state somehow. I felt Bishop Carpenter's mammoth hands enclose my scalp. On his right hand he wore the bishop's ring, an imposing amethyst stone set in a richly engraved solid gold setting. I could feel the bump on that finger as it encountered my head. When he got to the "more and more" part, he bore down so hard on my brain that I thought I might collapse onto the altar cushion from the sheer pressure. Bishop Carpenter may be one of the only people in captivity who could make "more" into a two-syllable word of major significance and magnitude. But something profound happened to me as he kept his big old paws fixed onto my skull. I wanted desperately to do just as he said, to "increase more and more" in those strange qualities he had listed as possibilities for my spiritual growth.

As he took his hands away and moved to the next person, I gave myself over to the moment. In that moment, I did not feel estranged or judged as too "different" to belong. Rather I felt close to Jesus, close to God, and far from my painful inability to be popular with schoolmates. The connection I experienced then was vastly different from what I felt at my own dining room table, where we talked and talked, but never seemed to say important things. What the giant minister spoke about in albeit general terms was exactly what was beginning to rumble around in my head, the head that had just had special hands laid so insistently upon it. His words also echoed questions I was beginning to entertain in my heart. How did I set out increasing my closeness to the Holy Spirit? Was the Holy Spirit like the "ghostly strength" he kept saying as he confirmed each of us? Was that Holy Spirit a ghost from heaven rather than a graveyard or scary story book?

———

As I became aware that I was not popular with my junior and senior high school classmates, I retreated ever further into books. Boys found me too much of a "brain" and girls tired of what I could talk about since it never was about "making out" or what I was going to wear to the Friday night football game. Mostly I read novels and some simple poetry, but one other book that came to attract me was Sir Thomas Cranmer's *Book of Common Prayer*, written in the 16th century. Initially, I was drawn to the short prayers called Collects. Wondering initially what that word might mean, I consulted my big Webster's Unabridged Dictionary and found this: "A short, comprehensive prayer, adapted to a particular day, occasion, or condition, and forming part of liturgy." Ever the word hound, I then had to look up "liturgy," since that was not in my vocabulary. Though my rector never did anything as formal as suggested by the definitions of liturgy, he did read collects every Sunday. But his were the ones stipulated for that particular day in the worship calendar. Often bored by a sermon, I began to explore the maroon prayer books in the pews, discovering at the back a passel of "collects" that came to fascinate me. My favorites, directed at specific groups or conditions, included those for sailors, rain, prisoners, people we love, and children. Phrases like "O eternal God, who ... rulest the raging of the sea," "Relieve the distressed, protect the innocent, awaken the guilty," "knowing that thou art doing for them better things than we can desire or pray for," and "O Lord Jesus Christ, who dost embrace children with the arms of thy mercy" became as familiar to me as "Jack be nimble, Jack be quick," or "Mary had a little lamb, its fleece was white as snow." Sometimes Mamie and I would read a few collects to one another before we went to church since she believed in getting into the right frame of mind so that we could get the most from our hour in the pew. (And it was "the" and not "some" pew. In church, my mother expected to sit in the third row on the leftmost aisle. Everyone else seemed to know that, because no one was ever occupying that space when we entered the back doorway and made our way to "our" seats. Similarly, at movie houses in Birmingham, which we frequented more often than we did Christ Church, Mamie always sat in the sixth row, again on the aisle. She claimed that sitting anywhere else altered her entire experience of the film. (I can only assume that my mother's experience of God would have been similarly altered if that third row pew had been taken.)

As I muddled through my teenage years, different collects began to command my attention, ones speaking to more abstract conditions rather than to specific occupations or individuals. Here, my two favorites were the collect to say at night and the collect for guidance. I memorized both so I could say them as I drifted off to sleep in the former case and whenever I felt the need for divine assistance in the latter. I still know them: "O Lord, support us all the day long, until the shadows lengthen and the evening comes, and our busy world is hushed, and the fever of life is over, and our work is done. Then in thy mercy grant us a safe lodging, and a holy rest, and peace at the last" (Cardinal Newman). And "O god, by whom the meek are guided in judgment, and light riseth up in darkness for the godly; Grant us, in all our doubts and uncertainties, the grace to ask what thou wouldest have us to do, that the Spirit of Wisdom may save us from false choices, and that in thy light we may see light, and in thy straight path may not stumble." Thinking about each of these simple prayers, I can only speculate on the source of their deep appeal. By the time I was fifteen or so, I valued quiet, even solitude, though I certainly filled most of my days with feverish activity. I also had come to understand that some of the people I saw on downtown streets did not enjoy safe lodging or a holy rest at the end of their days. "Guided judgment" had helped me see social injustice; could it help me live a life that allowed for both activism and solitude?

I began questioning everything in my restricted world. Some of those were mundane: Why didn't we fly a flag on the 4th of July like our neighbors? Were there people who ate on paper plates with grocery store utensils rather than using delicate china and sterling silver at every meal? If I pretended to be "stupid," would boys like me more? Others were deeper and unanswerable: Why were "Negroes" so hated and feared by most of the white people I knew? Why was I more comfortable with people much older than I rather than with my peers? Why couldn't we ever talk about my father in the years after he dropped dead when he was fifty-six and I was only fifteen? Did my sister really like working at the public library and turning over her pay check to her mother? Could I go far away to college so I could have some breathing room from my mother who seemed to become increasingly overly-solicitous as I got older? Amidst all this questioning, I hoped to find wisdom somewhere other than inside my own over-worked brain or from the mouths of adults who were supposedly teaching me how to think and act but who seemed more intent on corralling me into narrower and narrower confines. Their lessons went against some unnamed grain deep inside, causing me to disobey their strictures and test their limits at every turn. The Prayer Book's collect for guidance, on the other hand, suggested that is was all right, perhaps even beneficial, to entertain "doubts and uncertainties."

Chapter 3
Learning About Faith

*W*hen I went off to the University of Alabama in Tuscaloosa in 1954, one of the first places I located was Canterbury Chapel, the Episcopal student center. The minister, Emmet Gribbin, was entirely different from Mr. Burton, the rector of Christ Church back home in Fairfield. He was younger, for starters, and he didn't pinch female bottoms as my childhood rector could be seen doing every Sunday as ladies left the sanctuary, shaking his hand but getting a quick pat or tweak just as they were about to exit. Because my father saw Mr. Burton touch Mamie in that way, he refused to have him in our house and often cursed him as a hypocrite. My mother took a kindlier approach, though she clearly disliked his familiarity with her and her altar guild friends. Mr. Gribbin began to show me how to think about communion by taking apart the words recited during the worship service. We did this during discussion sessions held on Thursday evenings. When we weren't looking at the structure of the communion service, we were debating important tenets of our faith such as the virgin birth and the resurrection. One day, as I was walking back to my dormitory from one of those night meetings,

I flashed back to my Baptist neighbors, the Rivers family on Holly Court, and smiled at the ironic twist my life had taken. I now went to church not only for Sunday services but mid-week as well, not to listen to rote prayers but rather to think through what my faith asked me to do in the world.

The first day of school my sophomore year, 1955, Aurthurene Lucy tried to register at the University of Alabama as the first African American to attend a white institution of higher learning in the South. As I recoiled from the scene on the main drag of campus, lined that day three-thick with angry white men given a paid holiday from the all-white paper mill and rubber plant, I eventually threw my textbook at one of them. He had just thrown his brick through the back window of our new dean of women's Oldsmobile. The dean, Mrs. Sarah Healy, was driving Miss Lucy to class in order to protect her from the mob. I had a crush on the new dean from Michigan, so I had acted spontaneously out of some misplaced wish to protect Mrs. Healy rather than to protest Southern racism. The moment my book left my hand, however, I knew I was in danger so I ran as fast as I could to the Episcopal chapel and huddled quaking in a pew until the kindly minister spotted me and came to sit by me. Mr. Gribbin tried to calm me by reminding me that, though everyone was a child of God, many Southerners were scared and confused, and so they acted badly towards people they did not know or understand. Being a judgmental late-teenager, I thought he was being abstract; I knew for a fact that those men lining the street could not find any other jobs than the ones they had doing dirty and smelly menial labor. They couldn't compete against blacks trying for the same jobs.

By the Thursday after classes began, the board of trustees was insisting that Miss Lucy leave the University. I asked Mr. Gribbin if he would focus on race relations for our evening's discussion. Offering no resistance, he began that meeting with a prayer not found in Cranmer's *Book of Common Prayer*. I suspect he himself had written it hastily between my request earlier that afternoon and our gathering at seven o'clock. We were smaller than usual, perhaps because some people were queasy about venturing out at night in the still-hostile campus environment. Though most of the men lining our streets had returned to work, not being able to take time off without pay, die-hards still milled around the student union and adjacent quadrangle. Mr. Gribbin's prayer spoke to the unrest all around us, asking God to calm those upset by Miss Lucy's registration and to help us students accept that God loves all human beings, not just white ones. Then we each were asked to say how we felt about what was happening around her attempts to attend our University. Several people, usually articulate and energetic, seemed suddenly tongue-tied, but I said, "They will make her leave on one charge or another, and then we'll all be white again. I don't think this is very Christian, since Jesus welcomed anyone into his midst who wanted to be there. Aren't we being hypocritical? I'm very confused."

One or two others agreed with me, the kindly minister talked about how societies tended to resist major changes, but our talk petered out earlier than usual. His final prayer didn't have much to do with the subject, though it asked us to pray for those "afflicted." I decided that certainly included Miss Lucy, and might mean all of us white people, even the men still lining our main street. This weak effort by a church leader to turn Christian teachings to some tangible problem in the immediate world led me to question, as I walked back to my sorority house, whether organized religion was capable of being socially engaged or radical. Hadn't Josephine, with her seemingly unconditional love, helped me far more to get to a place where I knew that what was happening on campus was wrong--that Miss Lucy had as much right to attend the University as I did? And, hadn't spending so much time with Josephine, while Mamie was at garden club or auxiliary meetings or shopping downtown, planted an albeit inchoate grasp of just how cruel conservative white Southern values could be?

My decision to deepen my participation at the Episcopal chapel set me apart from most of my peers, who were in active revolt against the religion of their own childhoods. They stopped going to church almost as soon as they arrived on campus and enjoyed making jokes or otherwise casting aspersions on God and "all that jazz." Maybe I gravitated to the Episcopal student center because people there accepted me for who I was, and I didn't feel like a social failure. As I let myself comprehend that I was not particularly interested in dating the boys I met at the University of Alabama, I threw myself more ardently into talking about, and feeling more acutely in touch with my spiritual self. I also found both comfort and intellectual stimulation within a religious setting. People engaged in the life of the chapel seemed not to have even an implicit social agenda as their ulterior motive. They were not there to find a "date," so I could be seen as an equal in terms of being serious about acting in accordance with my beliefs. I continued, however, to be avoided by the fraternity boys with whom my sorority sisters felt I was supposed to be going out.

One friend in college did not find my devotion to things Episcopalian ludicrous. Rather, seeing the centrality of "church" in my life, my sorority roommate began asking me questions about what went on at Canterbury Chapel, giving me a chance to see if I could articulate any of what I felt every Sunday. Dot had joined her local Baptist church as a child because, as she put it when I asked her recently, "The teacher kept praying for the 'one lost soul among us' and I knew that was I!" By her early teens, she knew she didn't fit in with the Baptist agenda, while she remembered fondly once attending a Catholic church with an aunt when she was younger.

Since Dot was popular with boys and well-liked by our sorority sisters, if she also wanted to kneel with me in prayer on Sundays and take part in our weekly explorations of doctrine, then my having faith did not have to be a replacement for human contact. So her growing interest in the Episcopal Church was a great gift at a time when I might have abandoned or repressed my faith in order to feel more like a valid person. I went to several of her confirmation classes, and we spent many a late night in deep conversation about precepts that were entirely foreign to Dot, coming from such a different background. I remember how puzzled she was when the idea that the wafer and wine somehow were to be seen as Christ's presence was introduced to her group, since if Baptists participate in any form of communion, they do so infrequently and in a distinctly tepid manner. They pass tiny chunks of white bread and little cups of grape juice down pew rows and say virtually nothing about what the act might signify. So Dot brought her logical and thoroughly Protestant mind to bear on the concept of wafers and wine magically "becoming" a replication of the Last Supper when Jesus instructed his disciples in how to commemorate his coming sacrificial death. My being able to share with her my long-held conviction, from the time of my own confirmation, that the eucharistic moment is to be taken as profoundly metaphorical was a genuine help as she wove her way through the maze of new theological concepts. When she was confirmed, I cried because I felt I'd been able to help someone I loved dearly find a spiritual place that was sustaining rather than irritating or empty. In her mid-seventies, she is not a faithful attendant at the local Episcopal church in the Dominican Republic where she now lives, but when we speak through the miracle of Skype, we often talk about our time at the University. When I told her recently about my including her becoming an Episcopalian in this memoir, she replied: "I remember loving the silence and the ceremony in your church, things that were entirely absent at First Baptist. I needed a church that allowed and encouraged me to think, and that is exactly what I found at the chapel on campus."

———

Having been awarded a Woodrow Wilson Scholarship as I graduated from the University of Alabama in 1958, I could choose my next location more freely than had been possible four years earlier when my father's sudden and unexpected death had quashed any hopes I had to attend a "good" undergraduate school, e.g., Duke University or the University of North Carolina at Chapel Hill. The choice of graduate programs was not entirely open, however, since my mother was ardently opposed to my going very far from home. Having majored in English, I chose Vanderbilt University in Nashville, Tennessee, because they had been the home of the Fugitives, who worked to make New Criticism a popular approach to literature. I also chose it because its geographical location was far enough away from Birmingham to make it infeasible to go home every weekend, but close enough to satisfy Mamie's boundaries— that I was not to go more than one state away from Alabama for graduate work because "who knows what could happen to you."

In the fall of 1958, Vanderbilt began a radical experiment of allowing female graduate students to live "off" campus, so I took up residence in an old mansion right across the street from the University. Though six of us lived there, I gravitated to Martha Jo, the one person who talked openly and easily about her religious beliefs. She was engaged to a sweet man attending Vanderbilt's theological school, who wanted to minister to a small congregation when he finished his course work. The three of us became an informal discussion group, and Bill encouraged us to read the progressive "new" theologians he was studying.

Because I had long believed that books offered me wisdom I couldn't find anywhere else, I jumped at his recommendations and began to read voraciously—Thomas Merton, Paul Tillich, Martin Buber, and Karl Barth. These men stressed that God was not housed in some sky realm, but rather was a force to be found in other people or within relationships. God was not just a figurehead elevated into some vertical realm far from us and our lives; he had a distinct horizontal manifestation. Buber's concept of "I and Thou" satisfied my burgeoning belief in a God who was intimately concerned with the world of human exchange. My personal favorite articulation was Tillich's powerful expression of God as the essential "ground of our being." These men tended to stress the need for Christians to go beyond professions of faith, to translate belief into action on behalf of others less fortunate than we. Finally, they stressed the absolute need not to consider one's own religious tradition as better or truer than anyone else's.

In addition to these contemporary theologians, other much older figures became known to me at this time, people called mystics. I'd not heard about mystics before, and their intensity called out to me. My research soon yielded work by two such people—saints Teresa of Avila and John of the Cross. John's idea of the "dark night of the soul" made perfect sense to me, as someone who was beginning to find paradox and ambiguity to be familiar thoughtscapes. John's metaphors about the need to descend into darkness in order to discern the tiny beam of light that, if concentrated upon, could become God, moved me. This idea spoke to my own more mundane experiences with thoughts and feelings deemed inappropriate because too "dark" and "serious" for someone my age—Why were we created in the first place? How could a loving God let innocent children die? John's conviction that we cannot hope for ecstasy unless we are willing to enter into despair appealed to my growing appreciation for contradictory realities. He also helped me deepen my empathy for what God endured in his time on earth as the human Jesus.

I came to prefer the Apostles' to the Nicene Creed because it said in clear terms, "He died and was buried. He descended into Hell and on the third day, he rose again." I could believe in a God who was determined to experience even the worst and scariest of human conditions—separation from God, which was my understanding of what Hell was.

As for Saint Teresa of Avila, her writings about her covertly erotic unions with God awoke deep desires in me for total oneness with another being. From an early age, I was a romantic at heart, so stories like *Wuthering Heights* satisfied my own longing to find the person with whom I could feel as joined and "one" as Cathy did with Heathcliff, even if it were destructive. Teresa's ecstasies over seeing, and even being spoken to by Christ seemed entirely plausible to my imaginative self, so I thought, not for the first time, about entering a nunnery. Of course, I had no idea what that really entailed, since I wasn't even a Roman Catholic. Since the word "lesbian" was not in my lexicon, my toying with religious life could not have involved any conscious preference for an all-female milieu. Rather, when I was about ten years old, my mother had spent time in a Catholic hospital in Birmingham having a breast biopsy. When I visited her, the ward sisters, dressed in full traditional habit, smiled serenely at me. These seemingly benign women spoke in hushed, sweet tones, telling me my mother was fine and would soon be going home to take care of me, that I should pray to the loving Jesus to help her get well even more quickly. By the time of my year at Vanderbilt, as I became engrossed in the works of Teresa and John, being a nun also seemed desirable because you never had to think about what to wear to attract some boy's eye, nor did you have to try to make inane conversation with boys unable to talk about secular writers, much less religious ones. So I, as some noble women during medieval times, might have taken orders so as to avoid the heterosexual role of wife and mother, even as I told myself I was motivated by an ecstatic calling to renounce the world for God.

On the recommendation of one of my professors, I made time in my regular study schedule to read Marcel Eliade's *The Sacred and the Profane*, a work in which he decries the eventual separation of these two crucial aspects of life. Eliade's radical assertion that for centuries humans did not draw a sharp distinction between these two realms within their cultures reinforced my own inchoate ideas about the relationships between my body and my soul. I was beginning to perceive parallels between a person's developing sexuality and their theology, vaguely perceiving what many speak of as the sacredness of the body, not just as a temple for God's holiness to manifest itself but as a sensual locus of pleasure and union with another human being.

My spiritual life in Nashville was also strengthened and expanded by time spent with Malcolm, one of my fellow graduate students in English. Very tall and very handsome, Malcolm sported a healthy beard that he kept beautifully trimmed. He was a poet who had read more of St. John of the Cross than I had, though he was not familiar with St. Teresa. I think I fell in love with him, though the fact that he was seriously engaged to someone back in his home state suggests a convenient if never-stated "cap" to what might happen between us. We spent countless hours together, talking about T.S. Eliot and Robert Frost, as well as what we believed about God and Jesus. Our meetings often took place at the Episcopal Center on campus, presided over by a highly intellectual man named Stan and his kind, efficient assistant, Dot.

Stan recognized early on that Malcolm could hold his own about theological matters, so he began giving him books that we both read and debated. Several of these works dealt with the perennial conundrum that existed around the nature of Jesus. Malcolm believed that he was fully human and fully God and that there did not need to be any anxiety or conflict in that view. I tended to think of Jesus as a special prophet, wiser about the ways of God than even his friend, John the Baptist, and I didn't parse the "fully God" part of the argument. Maybe what caused me pause was a system of accounting in which one young girl named Mary plus an angel offering her a beautiful white lily could result in childbirth. Or maybe it was the simple fact that I too could become pregnant, but only through sex with a man. Whatever the cause of my hesitancy, Malcolm presented me with copious arguments not just about the fact of Jesus' being both God and man, but about the necessity of believing this if I wanted to count myself a sophisticated as well as a devoted Christian. Since Stan never offered me any books to read in order to increase my knowledge about theological matters, it was important to me to try and "measure up" intellectually, so I read whatever Malcolm passed along to me.

In our avid pursuit of the spiritual realm, we did things like climb the seldom-visited bell tower of the main Episcopal church in downtown Nashville. Full of cobwebs and bird feathers, the winding staircase was tricky under foot, but I made it to the top where we surprised several pigeons who flew at us and then sharply all around us in their eagerness to get out of what was surely their space invaded by us strangers. We both attached significance to the birds, and Malcolm subsequently wrote and dedicated to me a poem titled "The Belfry" about the experience. We also attended prayer services most weekday evenings at the campus chapel. These services lasted only about half an hour, involved a single hymn, a short reading from the Bible, and collects appropriate for the end of a busy day. I squeezed in these services, staying up later in order to get my academic work done, because I was centered and renewed every week, listening to and reciting the same healing words. By the end of that year, I could recite most of the words in the Evening Prayer liturgy. This service is a beautiful and simple experience, beginning with the general confession spoken by all present: "We have erred and strayed from thy ways like lost sheep. We have followed too much the devices and desires of our own hearts…. We have left undone those things which we ought to have done; and we have done those things which we ought not to have done; and there is no health in us." After that last powerful sentence, the prayer turns as we ask God to forgive us and help us lead better lives: "But thou, O Lord, have mercy upon us, miserable offenders. Spare thou those, O God, who confess their faults. Restore thou those who are penitent." A lesson (or sometimes two) is read by the minister, followed by one of the stunning canticles which include the Magnificat and the *nunc dimittis* from the gospel according to Luke. The more I spoke the words about Mary's accepting the visit from that angel with a lily, the more my heart opened to the possibility of miracles.

I always hoped we would say or sing the latter because doing so brought me amazing inner peace: "Lord now lettest thou thy servant depart in peace, according to thy word. For mine eyes have seen thy salvation, which thou hast prepared before the face of all people; to be a light to lighten the Gentiles, and to be the glory of thy people Israel." What moved me in those words was the quiet assurance that lay within that asked-for peaceful departure from where we were at that very moment, as well as the certainty that my eyes had seen the Lord's salvation. I couldn't have told you what I thought that last phrase meant, but repeating it several evenings each week gave me a vague sense of certainty. A recital of the Apostles' Creed was followed by several collects for peace or against perils or for the President of the United States, or for all conditions of men [sic]. At the very end, the minister stood facing us to say St. Chrysostom's plea: "Almighty God, who has given us grace at this time with one accord to make our common supplications unto thee; and dost promise that when two or three are gathered together in thy name thou wilt grant their requests; fulfill now, O Lord, the desires and petitions of thy servants, as may be most expedient for them; granting us in this world knowledge of thy truth, and in the world to come life everlasting."

———

Stan and Dot, who ran the Episcopal student center at Vanderbilt University, taught me a more pragmatic aspect of practicing my faith than I'd been able to achieve before that time. They organized us students into teams encouraged to take actions in the name of Jesus. Some of us visited the sick in a local hospital; two teams went a few miles out from town to hold prayer services in a local prison; because I had a car, I was encouraged to join a group that took healthy lunches to old people who were home-bound because of physical health problems or because they got "lost" if they ventured into the streets. Periodically we all met with our leaders to share our experiences and to hear them put those mundane behaviors into a long and deep tradition dating back to Christ and the Good Samaritan. In his sermons, Stan often talked about Jesus the healer, or Jesus the champion of the down-trodden, or Jesus the lover of all souls, no matter how shunned by society or officialdom.

The summer after my course work was completed, I stayed in Nashville, partly to avoid the hot-house atmosphere at home that my mother and sister thrived upon, but also to finish writing a Master's thesis on John Keats' *Endymion*. This long poem is about a shepherd who falls in love with the Moon goddess, who returns the feeling, though from quite a different plane. The crisis in the poem comes when Endymion, the shepherd, who has asked to cross the boundary between the human and the godly so he can be with his beloved, is told he may achieve this liminal state if he is willing to relinquish his humanity. After much angst expressed in beautiful blank verse lines, Endymion decides to remain human and endeavor to appreciate and perhaps even love the shepherd girl who already loves him in more familiar ways. I wanted to write about how this poem mirrored my emerging sense of my own choice to stay focused on tangible expressions of spiritual union with the unseen and unseeable, but my two faculty advisors made it completely clear that any such "personal" approach was unacceptable. Instead, I wrote about how Neo-Platonism informed Keats as he composed this work. My research was into Plotinus rather than justice theology, with the resulting thesis containing virtually nothing about how I myself shared just a little of Endymion's dilemma and found his choice to stay human a helpful mirror of my own efforts outside the restricted world of the English Department.

———

Having managed to please my two sparing advisers and get my Master's degree, I took my first position as an English teacher at an Episcopal high school and junior college for girls located in Vicksburg, Mississippi. Neither my interest in theological matters nor my devotion to the church played into my winding up at such a location for my first real job. Rather, when I registered with a job placement agency in Birmingham, the school in Vicksburg responded positively and, since there were no other openings, I simply took the job. In those days, no one had face-to-face interviews or visits to potential employment locations. The staff at the school and I chose each other sight unseen. But a lot happened in the two years I was there between 1959 and 1961. I learned that I was a very good teacher, able to reach students who were convinced they didn't like literature or that they were too stupid to understand it; I discovered that I loved women; I formed deep bonds with two other teachers more or less my own age, upsetting my usual failure to make friends except with very young children, animals, or people much older than I; I sank further into alcoholic drinking, behavior begun in my freshman year in college, as I struggled to grade more than 75 papers each week. But two contradictory things happened that influenced my understanding of the relationship between observance of religious ceremony inside church buildings and my own developing concept of faith: I got to help make worship services happen by serving as an acolyte; and I learned that some priests were "in it" for personal aggrandizement and ego-inflation.

Located in Vicksburg, All Saints' Episcopal School had a student population made up largely of boarders from Southern states. A few students came from other parts of the country, and another handful lived at home. They were usually quite bright intellectually, though often unstable emotionally, since in many cases, they came from homes where parents were divorced or, worse, continuing to live together in a state of hostility. There were three priests who either taught at or administered the school. The head was a man in his early forties who resembled most of all a large bull-dog. When he celebrated the Eucharist, he artificially intoned the words I so loved to hear, making it hard for me to find God within their cadences. I felt there was no room left at the altar—Father Jones took up all the space and was a clear example to me of the fallible human messenger of the sacred life of Christ. The second priest was a slight, fastidious, and intense person who was academic dean when not teaching secular and religious history. Father Wadenious would prove to be a staunch advocate in my case, even as the head would try to fire me during my first spring on campus. His devotion to the church seemed more intellectual and aesthetic than emotional, reminding me of the Prioress in Chaucer's *The Canterbury Tales*. Like her, he spent much time on his appearance and, like her, he relished a sumptuous meal or a glass of imported wine sent him from some large city in Texas.

The third cleric was a dear and devout man from Mexico, Father Bartolemo. His English was rough and his person usually disheveled. But his heart was huge, and his love of God was everywhere evident. Some of my fellow teachers and many students made fun of him because of his pronunciation of certain English words, but he was my favorite. His celebration of the Lord's Supper (he was too down-to-earth to call it the Eucharist) was the antithesis of Father Jones' self-important mouthing of beautiful words. Father Bartolemo clearly believed he was in the presence of his savior who had sacrificed his life so that we humans could live more abundantly. My defenses of him fell largely on deaf ears, but I always felt spiritually renewed after one of our albeit short conversations. He had a large family living in Mexico whom he missed terribly, whose pictures he never tired of showing me. When his little son was born, he came to me, beaming all the while, to show me first photos. The tiny male face wore a smile just like his kind father's.

Without realizing it, I was being exposed to a spectrum of God's servants. My reactions to each of them was immediate and sustained for the duration of my employment at All Saints'. I felt respect for Father Wadenious' intellect and advanced degree of cultural sophistication; I felt blessed by Father Bartolemo's simple faith; and I felt offended by Father Jones' ambitious "use" of Christianity to feather his own distinctly secular and power-based nest. Years after I had left Vicksburg, I would read without surprise that he had become first the bishop of a large diocese in Mississippi and eventually Bishop of the entire Episcopal hierarchy. His time at the girls' school in Vicksburg clearly had served as the launching pad he needed.

Students and faculty were required to attend "chapel" for Morning Prayer. Every week day, a sanctimonious woman with the title Dean of Students stood at the back of the church with her clip board and ballpoint pen, checking off names of any of us teachers not kneeling in a pew. I don't have any idea what happened to students who were absent, but if we faculty members missed a service we were called into the clip board wielder's office and given a tedious lecture on setting moral examples and fulfilling the spirit of our contracts. The three priests alternated in leading us; there was no music sung or even candles lighted; so the whole affair lasted only about twenty minutes, right after breakfast. Because I found Morning Prayer a good way to begin my work day, I wasn't tempted to skip chapel to have one more cup of strong black tea.

Sunday services were not required, but many who lived on campus attended. One of the two music teachers played the organ so we could sing, a sermon did occur, and the celebrant was usually either Father Wadenious or Father Jones. I assume they kept this duty from Father Bartolemo out of their own prejudices against his accented rendering of the words of the Communion service. Most Sundays found me in the congregation, though occasionally I "slept in" and had a leisurely breakfast with some of my colleagues who were doing the same.

Evening Prayer was neither required nor popular, since it coincided with one of the few "free" hours in the students' week days, and on Saturday they were too busy playing to pay attention to worship services. Because being in a sparsely populated chapel was at times the only "alone time" I had among so many young girls and the adults who tended them, most evenings found me among the scattering of people in the congregation. If a priest read the service, it was usually Father Bartolemo, since the other two men liked having some unstructured time in which to see family in the case of Father Jones, and to read at leisure in the case of Father Wadenious. Faculty were invited to read Evening Prayer since it contained no sacramental elements. After a couple of months, I screwed up my courage and volunteered to be the lector. Accompanied by about ten others on the Saturday late afternoon I first read, I was nervous but excited. I was about to be closer to an active religious experience than I'd ever been, and I even got to choose from among the lovely collects and invocations. My first offering of myself went smoothly, so I continued to put my name into the hopper as often as it seemed prudent, coming to appreciate the idea of a community of supplicants as I became their titular leader on many occasions during my two years at the school.

Because we only taught girls, there were not the requisite young males to serve as acolytes at the celebration of Holy Communion. Those in charge obviously had decided to bend the rules by allowing female students to assist, so at every eucharist, two of the girls found themselves at the altar, carrying cruets with wine and water, lighting and extinguishing candles, helping the priest wash his hands before handling the wafers. This visual difference registered with me and I found myself asking, at a faculty meeting, if faculty might also assist if they chose to. I wanted to do those holy things though I had no language of feminism yet in which to couch my request. Rather than invoking theories of patriarchal hegemony, my argument was disingenuous: "Wouldn't it be instructive to the students to see their teachers willing to serve as well as lead?" I asked. No one objected, so as soon as it became possible for faculty to sign up, I did so, always making sure, however, that the celebrant was Father Wanenious.

Standing so close to the altar was a strange and wonderful moment. Participating rather than passively watching made the act of receiving communion not just richer but also more tangible. Wielding the tall brass candle lighter, or being sure the handles of the cruets were turned just right as I offered them to the priest, or moving the chalice and paten from the altar to the little side table where they would sit until the service was over and they could be taken away and washed and put away—these simple, but necessary, acts brought me into closer contact with my idea of how it felt to be with Jesus in that original moment when he established the eucharist as a way for followers to feel his presence even when he was physically absent. I also understood without words that being an acolyte was categorically different from what Mamie had been about when she performed similarly "domestic" acts like polishing brass or washing linens or arranging flowers. Acolytes were male and altar guild members were female and somehow that fact alone allowed comparable actions to take on quite contrasting importance.

———

As I said, my years at All Saints were also the time when I discovered that I was a lesbian, though the word was not one I'd ever heard or used. In high school, boys kidded that anyone who wore green on Thursdays was a "fairy," but that was the extent of my exposure to the subject. It was 1960 in the South, and I knew very little about sexuality of any kind. During my first year of teaching, Maud, a young woman in my senior English class, began spending increasing amounts of time, first in my classroom and eventually in my living quarters at the top of the same building where all the residential students lived. Though only eighteen, she clearly had had much more sexual experience than I, though of course I was the more powerful because of my position. About midway into that fateful year, Father Jones called me into his office to say that a student had reported seeing me kissing Maud in the back of what we had thought was an empty chapel. Denying that charge came as second nature to me, since I had learned to lie-to-protect-my-skin when a child.

I dared the ambitious priest to have the accusing student do so to my face, so she was called into his office and asked by him to repeat what she had said to him privately. Perhaps the young woman valued what she was learning about English poetry, perhaps she liked me or her fellow student, perhaps she came to doubt her own eyes. For whatever reason, she was unable to charge me to my face. Watching my accuser struggle with what to say, I felt more immediate guilt for asking that young woman to deny her reality than I did for being in love with a woman, even one who was my student. The young woman's inability to repeat her claim made Father Jones look rather foolish for staging the scene, and I certainly relished that part of the occasion. That student and I never spoke about the incident.

Father Jones continued to haul me into his inner office, however, sometimes accompanied by Father Wadenious who always worked to defuse the situation. I remember one crucial meeting in the spring of my first year when Father Jones' spy, the woman with the clipboard taking faculty attendance at chapel, had reported seeing me talking or walking or reading in my own room with Maud. Jones was furious because I had not done as he ordered, i.e., stop speaking to the young woman except in class about an assignment. With a face reddened and blotched by barely contained fury, he sputtered, "I'd like to fire you now, but Father Wadenious says you are a fine classroom teacher, and we do NOT have anyone else to finish out this term, so I will let you stay. But if you keep up this relationship, you are 'out' at graduation." Graduation came very soon after that, and when Maud's parents came for the ceremony, and I was introduced, her mother gave me a tight-lipped smile, and her English professor father refused my outstretched hand. My first female love left All Saints' for college and I never heard from, spoke to, or saw her again.

Miraculously, Father Jones' attempts to humiliate me did not convince me that it was impossible to love women and remain a Christian. In fact, I was convinced that Christ would love me as he had all the pariahs who figured in so many of the miracle stories. Ironically, I believe the very lack of grim dogma within the historic Episcopal church also contributed to my being able to continue to participate fully in my faith world. In fact, as the pressures on me increased, I found myself on my knees more often than had been true in better times. I asked for the strength to remain true to myself and to what I was discovering about my own passionate nature.

While I was praying, however, Father Wadenious must have been working even harder on Father Jones because my contract was renewed, and I returned for a second and final year. I did this because I knew it would not look good on my vita if I only worked in my first real job for one year. A major change was in my living quarters. Many faculty lived on the top floor of the main building, which included classrooms, library, refectory, and rooms for all the boarding students. I had spent the first year in one such room, but found myself in the second fall housed in an ersatz colonial brick house, located many yards from the main building, where long-term faculty got to live. I suspect this isolation was part of the "deal" Father Wadenious struck to keep me. I lasted out the nine months, mostly behind the door of my room grading papers, and usually going out on Friday nights with two other women on staff to a local eatery for fried chicken, baked potato, iceberg lettuce salad, and three stiff whiskey sours. I also applied for the Ph.D. program in English at the University of Wisconsin-Madison so I could escape the world All Saints' represented.

At that school situated in the Civil War Memorial Park in Vicksburg, Mississippi, I learned about religious hypocrisy in members of the clergy, but I also learned that I quite adored teaching literature. Importantly, I discovered that I could find intimacy, both emotional and sexual, with women. Since, amazingly, this last "lesson" did not cost me my religious practice, I've thought often and deeply about how that could have been. After all, churches are still fighting over whether to welcome open lesbians and gay men into their midst as congregants and, especially, as clergy. One possible explanation may lie in the fact that my worship practices were grounded in that famous *via media*, or middle way, of Anglican and Episcopalian doctrine. This attempt to straddle religious controversy, beginning in the reign of Henry VIII when the king wanted to put aside his first wife for a complicated set of reasons, had given me a gentler view of God, Heaven, and Hell than was possible for people reared in strict Protestant or Evangelical faiths. Or, maybe I was determined to keep my God from agreeing with the likes of Father Jones or my Baptist childhood playmate, Sarah, both of whose religion involved more judgment than love. Maybe I thought that my God wouldn't stop loving me because I had found a way to express my own love, since "love" was the bedrock of Christ's teachings. Whatever the explanation, I packed up my dark green Volkswagen Beetle and drove as far north as I could figure out to go, my psyche battered but my spiritual self rather miraculously in tact. Surely there would be priests in liberal Madison, Wisconsin, who wouldn't hound me for who I had discovered myself to be in one important part of my person.

Chapter 4
Middle Exposure

*W*hen I left Alabama in the early fall of 1961, in my emerald green VW Bug loaded with clothes, books, LP records, and an electric frying pan given me by my mother so I could cook Southern in my apartment, I felt like I was embarking on a symbolic journey. Each mile took me farther from a South where my views of race relations made me a pariah to most who knew me, and where my new-found sexuality cast me into hell-fire. I became increasingly lighter-hearted as I drove through Tennessee, Kentucky, Illinois, and finally southern Wisconsin.

While I looked for an apartment, I stayed in the very small apartment of an old friend from the University of Alabama, who, amazingly, had chosen the University of Wisconsin for his own graduate work. Once unpacked, I went right out and bought a local newspaper so I could see what was "going on." The front page contained an article that confused and surprised me: residents on one of Madison's several lovely urban lakes had successfully barred an African American doctor and his family from buying a house in their upper middle-class neighborhood. How could this be happening in liberal Wisconsin? Was my home state and region not as benighted as I thought? Was the whole country benighted or worse?

With such questions whirling through my brain, I went to get food with a friend of my friend, who was hosting me until Joe returned from visiting his secret male lover who taught public school in a small town about an hour south of Madison. We went to one of the many hangouts on State Street, all of which seemed to serve only brats and beer to jolly students. As my eyes adjusted to the dim lighting, I caught sight of a heterosexual couple seated at the bar and excused myself quickly. I walked very fast to the ladies' room where I threw up. The couple was mixed race, an African American man with a white woman. For twenty years, I'd been told that such relationships would destroy the very fabric of civilized society, that the Bible had set apart the "children of Ham" as inferior in their darkness, and that sex with white women was what all "Negro" men thought about. While my racial politics were quite liberal, my visceral conditioning clearly had elicited an involuntary physical response to what I only knew to call "miscegenation," a long and ugly word not unlike "illegitimate," used to condemn behaviors deemed taboo by one's culture. Clearly, I had a lot to unlearn if I hoped to be accepted by the kinds of graduate students I wanted to like me. More importantly, I was going to have to work on the racist indoctrination that had clearly infected my heart in ways much harder to detect or alter than was the case with my head. I needed to unseat cultural dogmas and replace them with my faith in the power of love to refuse boundaries imposed by such dogmas. To do this, I would need to remind myself what I knew and admired about Jesus, someone who defied all cultural conventions by caring about those seen as so "other" as to be beyond acceptance.

If, during my first weeks of classes and teaching assistant orientation, I happened to mention my being an Episcopalian looking for a friendly church, responses such as "CHURCH! You still do that?" or "I stopped all that faith stuff years ago" told me that none of my peers was practicing any kind of organized religion. Conversations peppered with derision of Christianity as a retrogressive and confining structure that helped people keep their heads buried in the proverbial sand confirmed my suspicion that, in order to "fit in," I needed to keep my spiritual beliefs to myself. Resorting to the yellow pages of the phone book, I wrote down addresses for three Episcopal Churches that seemed within reasonable driving distance from campus and began "visiting" to see if I could find a spiritual home in this contradictory city where I would spend the next three years. The first two locations were flops, one because its congregation was too big, the other because the sermon was unusually boring. Both were as casual as my Southern parishes had been. Since I had come to crave more ritualized practices, I decided to keep looking, though my expectations had become somewhat deflated.

Happily, I found exactly what I was hoping for. The building was Gothic and beautiful; the priest was young and handsome; the sermon was riveting and replete with quotations from literature, ancient and contemporary; and the service was "high," meaning lots of candles, weekly communion, and incense on special holy days. I even thought a couple of the men seated in the row in front of me might be gay, so I thanked the celebrant, dressed in an ornate green chasuble and sporting a firm handshake and broad smile of welcome.

Quickly I became a regular at St. Steven's, discovering that Father Brad was eager to discuss the virtues of incense, bells, genuflection, and other "popish" elements of faith. Like the sweet rector at Vanderbilt, he conducted mid-week discussion sessions attended by a few faculty from the University, along with several older women I became quite fond of. We always had a reading, perhaps from St. Thomas Aquinas or Thomas Merton or C.S. Lewis or St. Augustine. One member of this academic group turned out to be a brilliant young assistant professor in the English Department, so I felt truly blessed. Gradually, Henry Hunter became a friend in Bascom Hall at the U, where I studied Milton and the Edwardians, as well as in the church undercroft on Thursday evenings, where I stretched my knowledge and comprehension of theological giants. An unusually tall, lean, articulate bachelor, Henry eventually revealed that he was thinking of leaving the academy for the seminary. He wanted to become a priest like his idol, Father Brad. (In years after I left Madison, I often thought about Henry, deciding that he was most likely trying to avoid knowing that he was gay, perhaps seeking refuge within the ministry where he could be celibate without raising many questions.)

As life would have it, two undergraduate English majors with whom I became quite close also attended St. Steven's and also found intellectual stimulation from its priest. As life would also have it, Father Brad was not a uniformly admirable figure. Though married to a lovely woman and the father of three delightful children, he had a proclivity for extending pastoral "care" into the sexual realm. I learned this when Eleanor, one of my new friends, confessed amidst much weeping that she was having an affair with Brad—she had dropped the "Father" sobriquet. My friend's telling me of this betrayal on the part of Father Brad catapulted me right back to the spiritual morass I'd experienced in Vicksburg: once again, a man of the church was acting in such a way as to push me away from the institution in which my faith was embedded. The painful difference, because it made any decision to stop attending the high church I had finally found all the harder, was the fact that this flawed priest had many more admirable qualities than Father Jones could have hoped to possess.

I decided to keep going to Sunday services, though I stopped participating in the Thursday night discussions, which meant I no longer was talking with other serious Episcopalians trying to work our ways through such thorny fields as the virgin birth and the place of women in the church. To my amazement, I would learn in late fall of my second year that Father Brad had "dropped" Eleanor and taken up with Ginny, her roommate and my other young friend. Both women saw me as a confidante who would keep what they told me entirely to myself. So I held in stasis Eleanor's pain at being rejected when she thought Brad really loved her and might divorce his wife to be with her once she graduated, and Ginny's emotional stew composed of elation at being with such a vibrant older man and guilt over having replaced a good friend as his latest trophy.

Prayer helped me keep both stories separate and be of marginal help to my friends. After each of them spoke to me about her time with Father Brad, I prayed that she might feel strengthened by her faith and that I might focus on her story without letting my feelings slide over into how my other friend might be feeling. This practice did very little to resolve my own dilemma, however. Because the two women swore me to silence, I was unable to speak about this conundrum with anyone else. The irony of the whole matter was not lost on me: I should have been able to take this painful emotional dilemma to my spiritual leader, but he stood at the absolute center of the roiling emotions in all three of us who were being toyed with by him. Though we never spoke about it, I believe Father Brad assumed that I knew of his liaisons, since he knew how close Eleanor and Ginny were to me. But when he preached one Sunday on the theological distinctions between love and lust, quoting one of his favorites, St. Augustine, I could barely stay in my pew. Hypocrisy had long been a quality I abhorred, and the further I went in pursuit of a Ph.D. degree in literature, the more I saw the depth of havoc it could cause. Of course, I'd read Hawthorne's brilliant examination of hypocrisy in *The Scarlet Letter* and I knew of Chaucer's distaste for his Prioresse because she behaves hypocritically. Just as certainly, I'd witnessed it from earliest childhood in the South.

So why did I keep returning to Father Brad's church when I had to labor against my disgust at his personal behavior while listening to him render the Eucharistic prayers and perform the Eucharistic acts? I believe it was the very Eucharist itself, heightened for me by my having finally located a church where those familiar and welcome words and acts occurred in a context that awakened all my senses. At one point I decided to confront him about the pain he was causing to one woman after another, not to mention his wife at home with her own possible feelings and imaginings. We even set up an appointment late for one afternoon in his office at church. It may have been intended in some much larger scheme quite unknown to me, but he called that morning to cancel the appointment and to ask me to reschedule. I never did. Instead I sat in his congregation almost every week for the next two years, though my attendance declined near the end of my time in Madison. I had a dissertation to write, a job to apply for, and a mother's death in December of my last year to cope with, so I told myself I deserved to sleep late on Sundays since that was my only day "off."

Each of these major emotional states would have been ample reason to seek comfort and advice from a trusted man of the cloth. Father Brad wore the right clothes and had the right inflections, but in no way could he offer me spiritual solace or stability. That I couldn't take him my deep grief over losing the person who had insured that I have a life in the Episcopal church as a child carried its own cruel irony. Furthermore, my academic life demanded focused energy from me to complete and defend my dissertation even as I was deciding which of the three offers for teaching posts I should accept. The result was inevitable: I buried my grief, drank a lot, and told myself I needed to keep "busy" so I wouldn't miss Mamie so much. When I did make it to St. Stephen's, I had to work hard to avoid thinking about what it was doing to my spiritual life to keep swallowing my distaste and anger as I was preparing to experience Christ's presence in the Eucharist.

What my decision to persist with this minister who so flagrantly broke cardinal rules of ethical behavior taught me was something that only has persisted and expanded in the years following my time in Madison. I learned, though I did not have the language to say so, an important fact: "church" is not the same as faith. I kept my focus on the parts of the ritual that strengthened my faith, and I let the failure to uphold tenets of religious practice within ministry recede from the center of my consciousness. Years after leaving Madison, I would come to see difficult connections between what Father Brad did and what I had done as a teacher, albeit young and sexually inexperienced, at All Saints'.

———

Joining the faculty of the English Department at the University of Minnesota in the fall of 1964, I discovered that none of my colleagues still practiced whatever religious affiliation had been part of their younger lives. My social world was carefully monitored, since I was closeted as a lesbian and was living with a woman who had left her husband and son in Madison in order to come with me to a new life of her own in Minneapolis. Our apartment happened to be just across a busy thoroughfare, Hennepin Avenue, from a major downtown Episcopal Church, St. Mark's Cathedral. Determined not to let Father Brad "win" completely by driving me from a source of intellectual and spiritual strength, I went to early Communion the first Sunday I was in town. In order to take communion more often than the first Sunday of each month, a person had to attend this early service which, in the Episcopal church, historically attracts only a handful of people: seven a.m. is just too early for most of us. As it turned out, St. Mark's was not any more formal in its liturgical practices than had been my original little church in Fairfield, though the building itself is commanding and aesthetically beautiful. After two or three Sundays, a very short, older woman stopped me on my way out of the tiny chapel where the service was held. She introduced herself by saying she'd seen me at the annual English Department cocktail party, that her husband taught Shakespeare there, and that she wanted to welcome me to St. Mark's. "You are in the minority at the University, of course. You'll find that your colleagues have decided they can't be bothered with the complexities and contradictions basic to any genuine faith." I liked "Bet," as she was called, immediately upon hearing that sentence. Though she was decades older than I, I hoped we might be able to discuss religious matters, since she clearly saw the value of ambiguity when dealing with the ineffable and the unknowable.

Within a short time, she had invited me and my partner to her home near Lake of the Isles, an urban lake around which live some of Minneapolis' wealthiest and oldest families. Her husband, Harmon, the Shakespeare scholar, was not present, so the three of us talked amicably while drinking tiny glasses of dry sherry. Eventually, the occasion for our meetings became Sunday lunch where my department colleague was present. These were awkward times for all of us. Not entirely comfortable with the fact that both his luncheon guests were women who clearly shared lodgings at the very least, Harmon barely spoke. When he did, if it were about Shakespeare or related writers, I knew to stay silent and look politely interested. We read literature entirely differently. Harmon followed in the literalist footsteps of E.E. Stoll, who insisted that the only reason Hamlet does not murder Claudius immediately, after the ghost of his selfish father tells him to, is that some thing or some other character stands in his way. A column is the problem in one scene, a prayer posture in another instance, an intruder on the scene in a third case—Stoll was adamantly opposed to any psychological explanations for Hamlet's reluctance. I, on the other hand, believed that Shakespeare would not have bothered creating a motive for murder based on columns or *prie-dieux*. Bet understood my deep disagreement with Harmon and so guided the conversation to safer topics. What films had my partner and I seen recently? Had we found the wonderful market right downtown where shoppers either came from Skid Row or emerged from their chauffeured vehicles to buy delicacies, such as individually wrapped pieces of fruit or gorgeous headcheese and fresh mutton, neither of which food items I had ever seen? We had found that market, and we usually could report on at least one good foreign movie seen at the film society on campus. It turned out that Bet loved movies but seldom got to see any because her spouse thought them a trivial genre unworthy of his time or attention. Eventually we began inviting her to go with us so she could see some of the actors and stories she read about with eager interest in the newspaper.

At Bet's request, I began attending the 9:30 a.m. service at St. Mark's so I could hear the dean of the Cathedral, who had a reputation for delivering superb sermons. Hearing him for the first time, I found myself in tears. Henry Hancock's sermons reminded me of John Donne's, preached at St. Paul's Cathedral in London to overflow crowds known to stand in the outer foyer under umbrellas if it were raining and the sanctuary were full. I knew all about those events since my dissertation had been on Donne's 157 extant sermons. What had drawn me to them, besides the fact that there was relatively no serious scholarship about them yet, was the fact that Donne used himself as his clearest example of a sinner who had turned back to God. Because Donne had been a poet long before he was the Dean of St. Paul's, his prose was peppered with arresting metaphors and surging phrases intended to force his congregation to examine their own sins and need for repentance.

No one's sermons in my previous religious experience had approached Donne's intellectual breadth or spiritual intensity, so I seldom missed a Sunday after my initial visit. At one point, the church began printing some of the Dean's work, enabling me to treat those treatises just as I had Donne's hour-long sermons. If a head minister at a major urban church could work so hard to preach vibrant sermons, perhaps it was not antiquated or fusty of me to have written about a comparably dynamic 17th century preacher. I found myself an eager member of a functioning congregation that valued tightly argued and mentally challenging discourses. My gratitude to Bet for introducing me to the Reverend Dean Hancock was enormous.

Though his sermons were tremendously powerful, Reverend Hancock labored under a serious fault, in my estimation. A slight

Welshman, he had been Dean of St. Mark's for many years. The 1960s, when I encountered him, found him unable to respond creatively to the topical world around him or to act on the deeply humane impulses he surely had. Fear gradually overtook him—fear and a certain distaste for the rapid loss of standards and conventions of dress, speech, and action. He didn't think it respectful to come to church in shorts, no matter how hot it was in our un-air-conditioned building. He never referred to important issues such as the burgeoning Civil Rights Movement, making his sermons increasingly remote from pressing realities of the day. As the 1960s continued to challenge all manner of conventional thinking, this fear of the world was reflected not only in his words on Sunday mornings, but in the church's growing insularity from the world just outside its doors. Dean Hancock began to insist that virtually all the sizeable budget for his church each fiscal year be spent repairing the slate roof, or tuck-pointing the stunning stained glass, or purchasing elegant, hand-embroidered vestments.

My attempts to by-pass the political and philosophical evasions of my beloved sermon-giver were doomed, even though I had not exacted the same involvement from John Donne when I wrote about his sermons. I could not divorce the cassock from the man, no matter how beautiful the cloth and needlework undeniably might be. I needed us to agree about how the church might interact with the world, and we truly did not. At one point, I visited another parish in Minneapolis, but found myself so missing Dean Hancock's sonorous voice and piercing diction that I went back to my church in the center of the city and hoped something would change. Occasionally, it dawned on me that I was repeating my behavior in Madison with Father Brad—I was refusing to allow the messenger to deny me access to the message.

Gradually, the Dean's sermons increasingly reflected his insecurity and dismay at changes happening around but not within him. He spoke defensively in his sermons about the primary role of the church in history as being to preserve symbols and principles laid down by Christ and the Apostles. Our definitions of preservation differed: I saw no danger in using Episcopal principles to assist with populations shunned because of race, class, sexual orientation, or political activism. Denying access to the church's powerful symbols to those kept outside the fold for these temporal reasons seemed to run counter to how Jesus interacted with his world. The Christ stories involved precisely that sort of expansive approach to the secular world: I wanted to ask Dean Hancock how he interpreted Jesus' forgiving any sinner who approached him, or what he made of the fact that most of the miracles described in the Gospels were performed on average or even sub-average citizens, not on the cultural or religious elite.

The more frightened the Dean grew, the more energy went into such preaching, and the more disappointed I became. My friend Bet, with whom I spoke about my growing discomfort, urged me to have compassion for the Dean, caught in a period of rapid change, confused about how to alter long-held beliefs in order to lead his congregation smoothly through such changes. I tried, but increasingly I squirmed in my pew as he went on and on about holding to the old ways.

In 1968, when Dr. Martin Luther King, Jr. was assassinated, I waited for one of the three clergy working at St. Mark's to help me through this devastating event. No sermons were forthcoming. The Reverend Hancock seemed oblivious to the brutal murder in Memphis, so I reread "Letter from the Birmingham Jail," and wept over the nation's loss. I also prayed for some direction for myself in the face of what seemed a giant step backward into a bigoted past that haunted me even as I made my way in a putatively more enlightened Midwest. But when Robert Kennedy was assassinated, just two months after Dr. King, I must have made an albeit unconscious decision to "test" the Episcopal church.

The Sunday following Kennedy's assassination, I showed up at St. Mark's, sitting, as my mother had done before me, in my usual place, six rows from the chancel and altar railing. Yes, like Mamie before me, I gravitated to the same seat every Sunday, so her presence continued to echo in my own choice. I don't remember the processional hymn or the appointed lessons. I was hanging on, waiting for words of consolation and direction in the sermon. When I saw that it was to be preached by an elderly canon who had delayed retirement twice, and usually only helped prepare and deliver the Communion bread and wine, I felt momentarily disappointed since we would not be hearing Dean Hancock's stirring prose.

This canon, who usually preached about once a month, mounted the steps into the pulpit slowly because of his age, and stood quietly before us. My immediate disappointment that he was not the eloquent, if socially conservative, Dean deepened into something quite different when the canon began: "I am sure you've heard a lot about Senator Kennedy's assassination from Walter Cronkite, so I will not speak more about it." Stunned, I thought "Cronkite is a fine journalist, but I need SPIRITUAL words, not journalistic reportage." The canon continued: "Let us pray for Senator Kennedy's soul." I wasn't worried about Senator Kennedy's soul. It was MY soul and the soul of my country that needed immediate assistance, since we seemed to be careening toward utter lawlessness and emptiness. Then the canon stepped over some invisible but strong boundary of mine, more crucial than Father Jones' ambitions to become bishop or Father Brad's sexual promiscuity. He said "I'm going to preach on the etymology of the word 'grief.' Its beginnings are in the Urdu language…."

Whatever came after that is lost to me forever because I felt suddenly as if I were choking. I was hot and cold simultaneously and knew I had to leave the church before I screamed. So I rose from my seat on the aisle of that sixth row center pew and walked the interminable distance down the long, narrow path to the back door and out into the air. My church friend, Bet, never asked me about my sudden absence from Sunday services. My life partner had chosen to be with someone else by this point, so I didn't have her to help me work through what may well have been a self-sabotaging decision on my part. Since none of my friends cared about religion, I never spoke to anyone about this traumatic event. For more than three decades, I simply would not return to a formal church service, though I would continue to make halting efforts to grow spiritually.

Chapter 5
Floundering

N ot going to church on Sundays left a huge hole in my life and helped me engage in spiritual self-sabotage. Twenty-seven years of structured sacramental worship meant that alternative modalities left me uneasy, unsatisfied, or just plain bored. I missed genuflecting before entering the pew, kneeling on the barely-padded wooden slats to pray, feeling the familiar and subtle build-up to walking to the communion rail to kneel afresh and receive the tasteless but mystical wafer and swallow the nondescript but healing wine. My anger at being betrayed yet again by ministers of my preferred denomination cut me off from a community I had long depended upon as my path to Jesus and God. For a few months, I faithfully read through the Eucharistic service in *The Book of Common Prayer*, but being part of my immediate community of worshippers as well as of that huge, world-wide "body" of the church was at the very heart of my Sunday experience. So gradually I stopped the lonely mouthing of words I knew by heart, since I came to feel more bereft while saying them than I did if I found something else to do between nine and eleven o'clock. Some Sundays I went to brunch at someplace special, but those outings came to remind me of what I was not doing and so I stopped creating false alternatives. There simply was no substitute for being in St. Mark's Cathedral.

A few friends who were not entirely secular suggested, once feminism was flourishing in Minneapolis, that I try that avenue to spiritual meaningfulness, while others assured me that visiting the Unitarian Church would let me be part of a group of like-minded people. Because it was only two Victorian mansions down the street from my apartment, I tried the Unitarian Church first. Indeed, I did find like-minded people, but it was quickly apparent to me that what I wanted from church attendance was not a stimulating lecture on how to be a better person and a chance to sing a sweet song about peace and love. My work place provided me with quite enough mental stimulation. It was my soul that was hungry, and talks about man's [sic] humanity or the beauties of nature or even the power of good works left me restless at best and empty at worst.

The feminists weren't much better, though there I at least heard people talking about God as something other than a "he" who lived "up" somewhere beyond our visual field. But the music was popular women's music, and the "service" was antithetical to what I was used to, charting unfamiliar ground because of placing women at the center of what was said and done. While I got goose bumps from singing Helen Reddy's "I Am Woman" at a secular rally or concert, feminist culture seldom heightened my sense of spirituality. Spontaneous sermons about God's being female might appeal to my political consciousness, but they could not answer the call within me for ritual and sacramental observance. These elements, so familiar from my earliest childhood, connected me to the mysteries of life and death common to many faith communities. My experiments certainly lent intellectual and political meaning to the weeks when I took myself to alternative locations. But none of those visits touched my aching for Thomas Cranmer's words in the *Book of Common Prayer*, central to the Episcopal church's worship practice. Nor did they speak to my sharp sense of loss of a community immersed in predictable and sustaining ritual observances.

What is it about liturgy and ritual, even as practiced in less formal ways, that is so central to my understanding of my relationship to God, Jesus, and my own faith? Predictable and repeated rituals help take me out of my self, something I pray to be able to do, even if for a few moments, as I enter the Basilica on Sundays. And I want to be taken out of my self because that self remains too small, too limited, too narrow. My sense of this limitation of focusing only on me is also the reason I go to literature, ballet, music, and the visual arts. Literature in particular invites me to have empathy or at least understanding of characters whose behavior challenges me because it doesn't conform to my own ethics. When I attend worship services, I definitely want to be relieved of my autobiographical baggage so that I can draw closer to something much larger and more mysterious.

If what happens in churches is marked by spontaneity, I am not challenged to drop my attachment to my own ideas and feelings; I stay strangely isolated even though in a space with other people. In a dependable liturgical setting, however, "I" merge with all the other individuals seated around me, and all of us are asked to relinquish self and become mysteriously part of a whole greater than the sum of its parts. Often, after I've received the eucharistic wafer, I look at the long procession of congregants as they move slowly up to the person handing out those tasteless little circles, and then back to their pews. I ask myself "What brings you here, Sunday after Sunday? Are you, like me, trying to dissolve into some spiritual union not only with your fellow worshippers but with our shared beliefs that are being reenacted for the umpteenth time? Do you, like me, imagine people quite different from us Minnesotans doing the same thing in their own geographical settings, so that our sense of unity is geometrically increased?"

———

There surely may be a connection between my inability to find a replacement for the Episcopal ritual at St. Mark's Cathedral, because I felt abandoned by that institution, and my failure to seek help for what gradually but ineluctably became a very serious drinking problem. Having begun to use alcohol in my sophomore year of college, by the time I arrived in Minneapolis, I understood that I was unable to control my use of bourbon to erase anxiety, dull my pain, and buffer even strong positive emotions. Many mornings, I waked full of will power and moral resolve: "I WON'T drink today." Some days I even managed to carry out that mantra.

But stringing together a series of such days became increasingly harder to manage. For a while in the late 1960s, I was a week-end drunk, holing up in my apartment and then my own house from Friday late afternoon until Monday early morning. Since that period also found me drifting in and out of sexual relationships with women who did not live in my space, no one actually "knew" about my drinking. I never missed a day of teaching from having a bad hangover, though certainly I felt foggy and lethargic most mornings.

When I made the momentous decision to stop drinking, in the fall of 1974, I also decided to begin telling friends that I was a lesbian, since I knew the statistics about the connection between alcohol or drug abuse and living in the closet about one's sexuality. For four long and fraught years I did not drink, and I did not check myself into any treatment program or attend any AA meetings. During this same period, a popular poster, in black and white, showed a cat hanging on to the edge of a fence with splayed paws showing every nail of its two front feet. Its head hairs were sticking straight up and the expression on its face looked like a scary Halloween mask. That's how my world felt as I tried to handle life without the numbing blanket provided by Jack Daniels or Seagram's Seven Crown if it were near the end of the month and my cash flow was running short. Ironically, I was being asked, during these four barren years, to speak to women in treatment at Christopher Street, a splendid program in Minneapolis for gays and lesbians. The woman who ran the female wing asked me to talk to her clients about various aspects of the flourishing women's movement. Since Minneapolis was a nexus of feminist activity, I was also asked to tell these recovering lesbians about some of the feminist organizations they might join. Anyone weaning herself from addiction to alcohol or drugs faces the reality of suddenly having lots of free time. Addictions are time-consuming, so stopping drinking or using drugs leaves one with hours and hours every day during which the urge to return to the familiar is acute and powerful. So I'd trot off to Christopher Street, and spend an hour with a group of lesbians just about to "graduate" from treatment. They probably saw me as a successful professional woman whose life was orderly and rewarding. Little could they know that I was spending most evenings, confined to my house with my cat, not actively drinking but also not really living a full life, unable to write what I needed to write in order to progress as a professor. I was also unable to make or sustain any genuine relational ties, since people took time away from my primary relationship that most certainly was with alcohol.

One evening, I had to wait to give my little pep talk to the treatment group because one of its members was getting an AA medallion to mark sixty days of sobriety. The person who presented her with her medallion spoke of how much fun the woman was having and about what a solid friend she was, now that she wasn't using. Much clapping and laughter followed the awardee's speaking about amazing changes in her life now that she no longer got drunk three or four times a week. Unable to avoid or deny the warmth and camaraderie present in that room, I suddenly "got it." There was a way to be sober other than the one that was exhausting me as I struggled each evening not to return to bourbon.

Within days, I had made an appointment with the director of Christopher Street so that I might enroll in their program. She listened sympathetically but, when I finished explaining why I wanted to participate in her program, replied, "Sorry, Toni, you can't come here. You have to go to a mainstream treatment program since I'm pretty sure part of why you've drunk so long has to do with your shame about being a dyke." Clearly she thought I had to sober up and come to grips with why I drank so destructively in a setting where admitting I was a lesbian would not automatically be supported by those hearing my words. Shocked but determined, I enrolled in an out-patient treatment program in a suburb of Minneapolis where my fellow alcoholics and drug users were heterosexual men with wives and children. And the administrator at Christopher Street was right, as I learned in a painful session near the end of the program where the lead counselor asked me to relate my drinking to my sexual orientation and I took a very long time to be able to say around the sobs "I've been told that lesbians are not human beings in the best sense; I just want to feel like a human being."

Getting sober had only meant I stopped ingesting bourbon in large enough quantities to block most feelings before they took hold inside me. Graduating from treatment and beginning a long history with Alcoholics Anonymous (AA) meant active work on reclaiming all those blunted and aborted feelings and then coping with them without the aid of instant and dependable oblivion. It also meant coming to grips with God after a long and lonely hiatus.

At first, I didn't want anything to do with the concept, since God's representatives seemed to have been too flawed for me to keep depending upon or learning from them. In my first all-women's AA meeting, there was an "old-timer" who must have perceived my struggle and decided to help me. After one meeting where I'd mostly cried quietly in my chair, she approached me to see if I'd like to go for a walk before or after our next meeting. Having been told in treatment just to say "yes" to invitations, since isolation had been one of the pillars of my previous coping mechanism, I agreed. On that walk, the fellow member asked if I were experiencing rebellious feelings about the presence of the word "God" in several of the twelve steps. Yes, I said, and told her a short version of why: I'd seen flawed Episcopal ministers behave in ways that ran entirely counter to Jesus' teachings; the institution of the Episcopal church had refused far too long to recognize women as viable ministers of God's word; Christianity had shielded and tacitly supported horrible movements such as slavery in the South and the extermination of Jews during the Holocaust.

It was her next comment that saved me: "Don't you work with writers? Don't you have one of them that you especially like or admire?" "Virginia Woolf" fell off my tongue easily and truthfully. "Well, then, Toni, pray to Virginia. Yes, get on your knees at night and pray to her to help you stay sober and become receptive to the program."

I did exactly that, feeling foolish at first but persisting until it seemed quite normal to invoke the name of my favorite prose writer. I asked Virginia to help me not drink when that option would spring into my consciousness as I faced various stresses in my work or personal life. When the English Department kept refusing to promote me to full professor, it was Virginia whom I read avidly and thought of intently in order not to travel by default to my local liquor store. After about a year of invoking Woolf as my Higher Power, I began just kneeling and praying, not "to" anyone—and eventually found myself able to say "God" without wincing inside or feeling like a hypocrite. The wisdom of Bill W. and Doctor Bob in their wording of the steps about God sealed the deal for me as I finally heard that it was to the CARE of God that I was to turn over my will and life in Step 3, and it was to a "God of my understanding" that I was to pray to have my defects of character removed in Step 6. Finally, it was to a "power greater than myself" with no proper name at all that I was to look to restore me to a much-needed but little-remembered sanity imagined in Step 2.

————

    Without knowing it, I had begun a ritual in what I deemed my secular life that would come to nourish my spirit. When we first got together, my partner and I both wanted to find alternative ways to celebrate certain national holidays, including Christmas. So we began having what we called our Solstice Celebration. On the Sunday closest to the winter Solstice on December 20th, we gathered a group of close women friends into our living room around a roaring fire. Each woman brought a candle to help light the event—no electric lights were in use during the ritual. She also brought something to throw into the fire, either to give to the great darkness if the offering were about something negative or painful in her life, or to give to the coming light if the offering were about something creative or otherwise positive. Usually our group numbered about fifteen, a few lesbian couples and the rest good heterosexual friends. Gradually, all of us came to feel that the year-end holiday season would not be complete without the Solstice gathering. As the group members became more familiar with one another, what was said and tossed into the fireplace became more intimate and powerful. People who might not even see one another all year were able to share serious health problems, major life changes such as divorces or births or job changes, and deep concerns about growing older. When my partner and I stopped being a couple, I knew I wanted to continue having a Solstice celebration. As I looked around my living room, I felt sustained not only by the women speaking about their year, but by the very act of our being there. As a newer member of the group recently said to me, "When I'm at the Solstice, I listen so hard to everyone else. Then I feel like a better person than usual; I feel transformed." At some point, I realized that within the carefully repeated format of this December ritual, I had achieved a degree of spiritual predictability that I once had found in an Episcopal church setting.

After about six years of sobriety, however, I realized that I was becoming more serious about working to know exactly what the "God of my understanding" might be. Surely not the blond fellow with the long white beard and flowing robes colored in Sunday school back in Fairfield, Alabama. Just as surely not the abstract "ground of my being" from graduate school days in Tennessee. And, sadly, not even the iridescent goddess offered by feminist seers in my Minneapolis community. Granted, the God I encountered in Cranmer's prayer book had been compatible, but without a church building where his beloved words were read aloud each Sunday, I had lost immediate contact with that source of comfort. Where, then, to find and incorporate him/her/it into my daily life and practice? A vacation taken with my life partner, also in a twelve-step program and with whom I was very much in love, provided me with one new possibility.

It was late summer of 1982, and we were on a driving trip across country. One of our last stops was to be Niagara Falls—from the Canadian side. My partner had seen them from the Buffalo vantage point many years before, while I'd only heard romantic and surely apocryphal stories of honeymoon couples' going over the falls in a barrel. I was excited finally to see the much-imagined spot.

We got into town in late afternoon, hot and tired, glad we already had a booking at a hotel. After some harried cruising along streets crammed with parked vehicles and lined with one small hotel after the other, we found ours. Small and attractive from the outside, it proved to be quite pleasant in our rather large room with a view of some beautiful birch trees. An early dinner of some kind of fresh fish and sautéed vegetables, and a stroll around a few blocks found us ready for a long sleep in preparation for our day at the Falls.

The next morning, we ate breakfast quickly and then set out on foot to find the park that served as an entrance to the falls. When we got to the park, sound was my first clue. I heard pounding, steady and ever-louder, until we reached a railed platform from which the falls were first visible.

Breath-taking was what they were. From the Canadian side, we could look across at the great Horseshoe Falls in New York as well as down at the cascading water that was the northern display. After a long time of marveling from afar, I urged us to pay for a yellow slicker each and an admission ticket that allowed us to go down a series of narrow, water-coated and moss-covered steps that ran behind the falls. My partner wasn't sure about this option, but I was drawn by an invisible but potent magnet. Most of the other visitors were children with reluctant but indulgent parents in tow, so the descent was full of youthful shrieks amplified by the excellent acoustics that set up chains of echoes around every exuberant scream.

At several points during the descent, visitors were invited to pause to look out at the falling water through tightly screened but generously wide doorways. Each of these break-outs was at a lower level, so the force of the water increased geometrically each time. At the third and final opening, we were quite near the bottom of the falls. Many groups, parents claiming exhaustion and children having lost interest, stopped shy of this last viewing area. When my partner and I arrived—I had of course insisted that we continue to the end of possibilities—we found ourselves virtually alone amongst a scattering of perhaps ten other die-hards, most of whom were without children.

This vista was set off not by the wide mesh netting used in the other instances; rather, a single iron railing held us back from the edge of the concrete slab and doorway that framed the window onto the water. The sound was almost deafening because of several hundred feet through which the tons of water had already plummeted. Data had told us how many tons were falling per minute and with what force. I no longer remember any of those scientific, hydrological figures because whatever they were is mere calculation. What I will never forget is the mystery and miracle right in front of me. From where we were standing in our drenched slickers, spray from the falls hit my face and body as I moved to the very last inch allowed to visitors. Pushing my body against the cold iron rail, I leaned toward the wall of water, wanting to get as close as possible to its force field and to its sublimity. In fact, my overwhelming desire was to merge myself with that water, to walk into the falls because God was there, potent but gentle, awesome but inviting.

My partner tugged at my yellow sleeve, smiling quietly, understanding my feeling but drawing her line in the falls-splashed cement about keeping me in the world of gravity and eventual dryness. More than thirty years later, I can will myself back onto that shelf, facing the most powerful display of sheer omnipotence I have ever witnessed. Surely part of the power of that moment lies in its connection to baptism by water as a sign of rebirth. I see this in my own gardens on a hot summer afternoon. Hooking up my sprinkler can cause wilting plants to raise their little thirsty heads after very short exposure to the balm of water. So my soul must have felt as I stood mesmerized by the sheer force of that cascading, life-bringing water. There's a hymn in the Episcopal church that comes to me in these reveries about Canadian Niagara. It affirms God in "earthquake, wind and fire," going on to name what is heard paradoxically as "the still, small voice" of that deity. I'd never fully grasped the truth within the paradox until standing before that wall of water that overwhelmed my senses and propelled me into an ecstasy of power and peace. Was this the way the mystics had felt when they were "visited" by their God?

My problem was how to translate the tremendous ecstasy I felt standing before that cascading water into more mundane practices that would engage my spirit. One such adaptation has been found in gardening. Some current eco-critics assert that gardens are totally domesticated nature, as far from genuine wilderness as a person can get. They associate sublimity with wilderness and contentment with gardening. Surely, my reaction to Niagara Falls involved sublime feelings, but so too are many of my reactions to digging and planting and tending my gardens. In both contexts, I have been and am able to lose myself amidst forces of natural beauty and regeneration. So for me, perhaps the categories of wild and domestic do not apply as cleanly as the theorists suggest.

When my partner and I moved into a wonderful old three-story house in South Minneapolis, built in 1911, we inherited a lot of yard with next to nothing planted in it. The family who had lived for many years in the house had sent four children to college on a skilled-worker's salary, so nothing had been done to modernize the inside of the dwelling or to beautify its outside. Shingles were blowing off the roof during windy late-fall evenings right after we settled in, and in the first spring of our living there, all that came up out of the earth were a few straggly tulips and a few pink phlox in the back yard. Both my partner and I loved to garden, but our first seasons were spent in literally bringing "dead dirt" back to a state that could sustain growth. Many bags of cow manure and peat went into that inert soil, and our second spring saw new, healthier tulips that we had planted the previous fall, acting on faith that they would reward us by actually blooming.

As we planted more and more perennials and designed places to put in colorful annuals, I discovered that getting my hands dirty in the garden brought me deep satisfaction. When we worked together, the garden intensified our closeness to one another; when I worked alone, I felt part of a force in the universe that was both ineffable and immediate. Soil and plants and bone meal somehow morphed into mystery and invisible, but powerful, cycles of growth and dormancy. Importantly, I also felt I could give myself over to whatever that force was without fear of being disappointed by heavy-handed sermons or angered by political systems that often excluded people like me. I was realizing that spiritual experience, for me, was in no way limited to institutional religious doctrines or architectural loci of worship.

This sense of the sacredness of growing flowers should not have surprised me, given a significant prenatal event in my life. Once my parents knew a second child was eminent, they had to move from the model home built by United States Steel in Fairfield, Alabama, to prove that working people could own and maintain attractive houses. The house they found, for the grand sum of $5,357 in 1937, abutted a vacant lot that no one seemed to have wanted to develop, so my mother, operating perhaps from some ancient notion of "squatters' rights," decided it was hers.

They took occupancy in late February, and I appeared on April 3rd, but Mamie was intent on planting late winter bulbs that might even come up and bloom their first spring in residence. So she took an old pillow outside to sit on and literally bounced down the gradually sloping hillside, planting hundreds of iris and jonquils with me quite developed inside her womb. Just as people play certain kinds of music to babies in utero so that the newborn will begin with a taste for those sounds, I believe my mother imprinted gardening on my very cells.

If going to Christ Episcopal Church with Mamie was the bedrock for my spiritual life, helping her in the garden seemed only to expand my sense of "where" God might reside. Again, paradoxically, that God seemed more accessible to me outside with the flowers than inside with the dressed up adults and boring minister. Again, I was preferring direct experience with a God I felt positively toward over dogmatic creedal systems, even though I had long found comfort within the formality of the Episcopal church. As I recall, my mother did not like weeding her huge garden just as she did not like washing up after her elaborate cooking ventures. So I became the weeder at quite an early age. In the South of my childhood, weeds thrived even more vigorously than in other parts of the country because they never completely died off during the winter. So from about mid-February when the snow drops first appeared under the magnolia tree, until well after Thanksgiving, I sat or leaned down to rid the beds of unwanted growth. In one of her many moments of wry wisdom, Agatha Christie's delightful Miss Marple says to someone ignorant of gardening, "A weed is just a flower growing where you don't want it to be." I often hear Miss Marple as I, now in my seventies, weed my own garden and ponder if God disapproves of my cutting short the lives of so many green things just because I've decided they don't "belong." In certain bare spots of the garden, not visible to most people, I occasionally let a weed stay for the entire season.

As a child, however, no such luxury could be mine. One weed in particular eluded me most often. It was dark green with a sort of bloom that stuck up and was covered at the end with hundreds of minuscule black dots. It may even have been some kind of coarse grass rather than the usual weed we imagine. I used the stalks to string four-o'clocks because all those little black specks kept the magenta flowerets from falling off the thin stems. But Mamie detested this invader because it spread fast and could literally choke her blooming things, so I was sent out to attack it with full force. Tiring of the tedious process of using a trowel to dig up the roots, I cheated when she wasn't nearby and just pulled up clumps so they didn't show any longer. Of course, they reappeared within a few days, irritating my mother who grasped instantly that my trying to cut corners was the reason. To me, it always seemed there were more after I'd yanked up a few strands, sort of like getting two worms when one is cut in half.

My favorite activity in the garden was working with Mamie to cut stunning iris for vases inside, and then to cut off the dead blossoms so the plant's energy could go to generating more buds. She often asked me which iris she should select for a special arrangement, so I learned the names of lots of varieties. Unlike some gardeners who believe it is wrong to cut flowers, my mother wanted to bring the fruits of her loving labor into virtually every room of our house, just as she insisted that we use the delicate china and crystal rather than "saving" them for company. This sense of using beauty everyday has stayed with me, allowing me to celebrate creation as part of my daily life. This makes me, in secular terminology, an aesthete. In spiritual terms, I believe it keeps me close to what I conceive of as God, the source of all creative impulses and achievements.

———

As months turned into years, my decision to stop going to church became a habit, though I continued to feel a void because I prayed, albeit alone. I occasionally remembered to read Cranmer's beautiful collects alone, and I struggled to hang on to my faith. With no familiar frame within which to explore whether my soul was alive and expanding, however, I believe the spiritual part of my nature stopped thriving because of my deep need for community and ritual. I began to wonder if it were easier for my friends who had grown up in non-liturgical churches to replace that format with ones more compatible with their present inclinations. Because such churches relied on spontaneity and individualism without any formal ritualized behaviors or observances, it seemed easier for some of them to "replace" their Sunday observances with other stimulating or pleasant activities. When I asked such people if they "missed church," they looked at me strangely and replied "Why would I do that? I now read the *New York Times*/ski with my family/go to the health club/have brunch at a favorite restaurant." These comments speak to successful adjustment away from childhood religious settings, an adjustment that my perennial wrestling with my Episcopal tradition and its meaning prevented me from making.

In about 1975, a little while after I stopped drinking, I decided to give the Episcopal Church another chance. Part of my gradual recovery from being an active alcoholic involved renewing connections with people or places I had cut out of my life, so including church seemed a logical path to pursue. Additionally, word had it that St. Mark's had hired a new dean from Texas who actually looked outside his beautiful building to see the people who spent their days in Loring Park, just across the street from the church. That meant he was seeing the single mothers with toddlers in strollers or playing on the dilapidated swings provided; he was seeing drunks and druggies sleeping off the night before; he was seeing prostituted women sunning themselves on rusting benches; and he was seeing gay men, many of whom were also prostituted, trying to show affection without being beaten up or hollered at by passersby.

Yearning to return to services that gave me spiritual sustenance, I decided to meet the new man, come out as a lesbian and a recovering alcoholic, and offer my services as a Sunday school teacher. Depending on how he responded, both verbally and with body language, I would be able to tell if we found each other acceptable. If he grew restless, for instance, or moved his chair further away from me, or stumbled over whatever he said in response, I would know not to re-engage. If he said something like, "I certainly endorse the idea of a 'big tent church'," or "We at St. Mark's embrace diversity," or, worst of all, "Thank you for your frankness, and I'm sure there is a place for you somewhere in our programming," I would once again leave a space that held no genuine relevance for me. Liberal slogans and mantras like these no longer held any weight with me. If, on the other hand, he "passed" my test by saying the word "lesbian" out loud, or better yet, seemed eager to have my services in teaching the young about Christian ideas, then I would return. Perhaps I might even find a way to connect with more members of the congregation, since originally I'd only gotten to know the sweet woman married to the procrustean Shakespearean colleague.

Two days before I was to meet with the rector, local television news reported that the association of Episcopal bishops, meeting in Boston, had voted for the third time not to allow women priests to be ordained. This repeated rejection of women as *bona fide* ministers of God's word hurt me deeply, not just because I was an ardent feminist. It hurt me because it said an institution I loved could not allow people like me to participate in all aspects of the church's mission; finally, the hierarchy could not take people like me seriously. I remembered learning somewhere that into the 19th century, people in North America were still debating whether women had souls. Why was I going back to a source of such pain? Surely there must be some venue where I could find genuine spiritual nourishment and succor for my spirit.

Next morning, I called to cancel my appointment. Maybe my hasty action deprived me of connecting with a minister who might have agreed with me about ordination of women and other justice issues, but keeping the meeting felt too much like going to a dry well hoping for water. Once again the structure of "the church" had betrayed me by refusing to see women as full participants. So, while the new dean of St. Mark's may well have been more connected with his immediate surroundings than Henry Hancock had been, I was still too hurt to re-engage.

Feeling angry and abandoned yet again by the church of my choice, I sought what comfort I could find in my AA meetings where it was at least possible to talk about God without feeling retrogressive or sentimental or worse, once I'd become able to say "God" rather than "Virginia." Having tentatively resolved some of my bitterness at organized religion, I began to feel a need for something more intellectually engaging than just reading the twelve steps each week. My spiritual yearnings were in conflict with my political beliefs, so I did the best I could at the time. I established a regimen that brought me tremendous spiritual calm and strengthened my sobriety along the way. Immediately after breakfast, I'd read the daily offering from one of AA's recommended "little books." Then I'd open my journal and write as long as words came, letting my mind play with phrases and ideas generated by each short but evocative reading. Since four out of five contained some reference to a Higher Power, that meant most mornings I got to reflect on my evolving sense of that being or force or reality as it might re-enter my life. The fact that I now have arrived at a place where I can handle ambiguity more adroitly, I am able to be an active part of a congregation that, while a part of the Roman Catholic faith, straddles its own contradictions between personal belief and formal dictates.

Reading over some of those journal entries shows me how much I yearned for a spiritual home, a place where I could stand (and kneel) with others rather than continue my lonely pursuit of God. In retrospect, it seems that I may have stopped my daily reading/writing practice precisely because it deepened my sense of spiritual isolation. At moments, even as I wrote eagerly in my journal about some phrase in that day's readings, I felt like a spiritual orphan. My entries gradually became first shorter in length, and then they occurred less often. Finally, they gave way to more secular and mundane matters such as my struggle with overeating or my efforts to express deeper feelings to my partner than had been possible for me in the past.

It was during the period of writing about reading that I realized that something was changing about my ability to relate directly to "God." Like all my "awakenings," there were no flashing lights or sudden epiphanies—my light-bulb moments usually resemble an emotional rheostat rather than a panel of floodlights. (Moments of ecstasy like those I felt at Niagara Falls have been very few in my life.) But when I registered my loss of verbal resistance, I wrote about that, realizing that Virginia Woolf had served as a crucial place-holder while I hewed out the beginnings of a new idea of God.

From then on—it was the late 1980s—I flirted with returning to some organized religious setting. For a while I visited Episcopal churches in the Twin Cities, always with my partner who had long ago left her fundamentalist Baptist background, but was generous enough to accompany me on several forays back into organized religion. I soon discovered that my church had put Cranmer's *Book of Common Prayer* on a theological shelf somewhere and was now using a "modern" rewording of the stunningly beautiful services of morning and evening prayer, as well as holy communion. What was being said at the altar hurt my ears, distracting me from any hope of a meditative hour. We no longer gathered together in "Thy" name; now it was "your" name. No longer did we reply to the celebrant's "Let us give thanks unto the Lord our God" with "It is meet and right so to do." An editor in a cubicle at some religious publishing house had decided we should say that it was a good thing to give thanks to God. What did all this emendation that stripped the language of its former poetry signify? Was it possible for my church to retain and celebrate the best of tradition even as it embraced new strands of belief and practice?

I am not someone averse to or frightened by change; I have

marched and lobbied for new laws and procedures to allow us to acknowledge and even affirm our present-day world. Like Edmund Spenser, who wrote his *Mutability Cantos* at the end of the 16th century, I acknowledge that the only true certainty in our lives is the inevitability of change. So why does it so rile my consciousness to have the language with which I am familiar replaced by what seems flat and uninviting? On one level, the answer is simple: for over fifty years, I have taught literature that depends for its power on just the right combination of words. So language is of paramount importance to me. But this is not enough of an explanation for the depth and intensity of my feeling about what is said in a worship service. Surely, these words have deeper weight for me because they were my initial entry into relationship with the ineffable, my best route to God. Sixty years after first listening to and saying Cranmer's words, I can and do recite them when trying to sleep or caught in traffic or simply wanting to feel the secure calm they inspire in me.

Irritated and saddened, I telephoned the central Episcopal office serving my diocese, asking if any church in my area still worshiped using an unaltered version of *The Book of Common Prayer*. There was one, so my partner and I drove over to St. Dunstan's church in St. Paul to let me witness the beauty of my beloved words. For the hour of the one communion service I attended at that "traditional" church, my heart was warmed by hearing the familiar words and cadences. Unfortunately, retaining Cranmer's version of the liturgy came in a constellation of retrograde practices. Not a single female person took part in the service—no woman read either of the Biblical selections appointed for that Sunday; no woman served as acolyte to provide water and a little towel to the priest as he readied himself for the re-enactment of the Last Supper; no woman carried the cross or the single brass candle holders; no woman circulated the offertory baskets; no woman even handed out the bulletin in the narthex before the formal service began.

Clearly I was not going to be able to find a "place" within the Episcopal family, even though women were being ordained in ever-greater numbers. I even knew of one such woman, a student during my first years at the University, who for a time was part of the staff at St. Mark's Cathedral where I had originally worshipped. Feeling loyal to her, I found out which Sundays she would be preaching and attended several of those services, trying to ignore how discordant most of the words had become. But something shadowed those visits, making them unsustainable; if I were going to reengage with some church, it was going to have to be one that did not remind me so forcefully of flawed messengers.

———

While I was floundering about trying to locate a house of worship that felt welcoming or at least possible, my partner was on her own faith journey. Deeply musical and a veteran of various church choirs from her childhood years through college, she had discovered that the Basilica of St. Mary, on the edge of downtown Minneapolis, had one of the finest choirs in the region. Directed by a woman graduate of St. Olaf College, known for its superb music department and for its multiple choirs, the Basilica group demanded auditions of its potential members before being accepted into its ranks. As soon as my partner retired, in 2000, she scheduled such an audition to see if her alto voice was good enough. It was, and she began a satisfying experience at the Basilica singing, becoming part of the choir family, and eventually managing the music library which became the equivalent of a part-time job.

At first, I attended Sunday services reluctantly, since I had little use for the papacy with its ultra-conservative and unloving stances on many issues. I believed that women should be allowed to become priests, and I was deeply offended by the Church's official position on a woman's right to choose to terminate an unwanted or ill-conceived pregnancy. Most certainly, I rebelled against the Pope's periodic encyclicals inveighing against "homosexuality" as an abomination against God. But my partner wanted me to hear her singing, to be part of such an important element that was coming back into her life, so I attended Sunday services probably once every couple of months. As we would ride home from these events, I'd often talk about aspects of the liturgy with which she was unfamiliar, given her conservative Baptist background. We laughed that she was the newly confirmed Catholic, but it was I who could explain central ideas such as transubstantiation, the Ascension, or the role of saints in daily prayer life.

What I encountered at the Basilica mass ritual was familiar, reminding me of the "high" Episcopal church I'd found years before in Nashville. Though I missed Thomas Cranmer's prose, there was incense and lots of candles, and, on festival days, beautiful banners, adorned with tiny bells that tinkled as the carriers processed down the aisles, bringing positive chills down my spine. Music from the choir was always its own beauty, often profoundly moving, especially when they sang something in Latin. And, since Cranmer was not part of traditional Roman Catholic liturgical language, I was able to stay present to what was happening in the huge and gorgeous basilica building rather than lamenting or begrudging absent phrases that had sustained and challenged me for so many years.

The rector at the Basilica of St. Mary, Father Michael O'Connell, was a progressive man who spoke in more than one of his homilies about his own recovery from years of alcoholic drinking. On one occasion, when an old friend of my partner's was visiting us, she and I were seated in the congregation when Father Michael preached on why it is doing Christ's will to welcome gays and lesbians to communion. He walked down to the rail that once would have been closed at the time of people's going up and kneeling to receive the host and wine, but that now remained a vestigial sign of older days in church history. As he spoke about the un-Christian nature of homophobia, he slowly closed the gate, being sure to help it clank shut so we could hear the sound of exclusion about which he was speaking. When he enjoined us to extend active welcome to ALL who wanted to share in the Eucharist, he unlocked the little gate, swung it open, and declared that the Basilica does not merely accept, but it values its gay and lesbian members. Applause broke out, originating in the choir stalls where many gay men and two or three lesbians were seated. Of course I joined in immediately as tears rolled down my face. Many in the large congregation clapped loudly, though I heard that Father Michael got a slew of telephone calls on Monday morning from outraged members who did not share his inclusive stance.

I felt at ease in the pews of my partner's adopted church and my partner clearly would have liked me to be there more often to hear the choir perform its moving offerings. Something in me rebelled against that, and a certain tension took hold between us. Maybe I didn't want to "horn in" on something she had found that meant a lot to her. Maybe I feared being betrayed once again by some aspect of organized religion. Maybe I feared the tears that came so quickly as I entered into singing the processional and recessional hymns or the responses during the preparation of the eucharist. Whatever the cause, if my partner suggested I go hear the music two weeks in a row, I'd usually make some flip remark like, "I've had enough of church for just now; later." Probably each of those quips stung her heart, but I needed to continue to protect myself against being betrayed yet again by a religious institution. At one point about two years after she joined the choir, she asked me one night at dinner if I believed in God. Stunned by the clarity of the question and puzzled by my hesitation in answering, I remember saying something feeble like, "I believe there is a force for good in the universe that leans toward goodness, and I believe that force can be present in all of us if we act kindly and with generosity toward those around us." It was a hedge and we both knew it, but it was the best I could muster at the time.

The year before my partner told me she wanted to end our relationship because she was in love with another woman, I was feeling more secure about going to church. I had told her early in that fall that I wanted to attend once a month so I could hear more of what she was singing. Before mass began on each of those visits, I'd kneel and ask to be able to remain open to what was going to happen during the service. That prayer must have taken root, because often I found myself weeping quietly but feeling supported as I listened and responded to the special musical offerings given us by the choir, or as I watched children carrying bowls of smoking incense as they accompanied those bringing wine and wafers from the back of the church or escorting the choir as they came and went. Sometimes I really was inspired by a homily, so in the car on the way home, we'd talk animatedly about implications of the message for each of us in our daily lives. Often I was more engaged in the content and ritual than was my partner, whose focus, understandably, was on the music.

It was September of 2005 when I learned that my partner wanted a divorce. Though we continued to see a sexuality counselor, whom we'd engaged in order to enliven that aspect of our shared life, I noticed that I was attending church services much more often than had been my practice. As my life unraveled that fall, winter, and spring, I got myself every Sunday onto the bus that ran near our house and then, twelve minutes later, deposited me across a main street from the church. I was using public transportation because we had gone to owning only one car once both of us had retired, and Sunday mornings were one of my partner's "times" to have our vehicle since she had to be at church much earlier than I did.

Maybe my frequent attendance at the Basilica was a repeat on a deeper level of what I needed but didn't get after the second Kennedy assassination. Walter Cronkite hadn't been enough then because my needs were distinctly spiritual. Now, I was getting something that helped me keep going at a devastating moment in my life, and, my value system has never included being a sponger or parasite. If I were going to attend the Basilica of St. Mary regularly, I felt ethically compelled to consider becoming a member of the congregation. Upon my request, someone quickly mailed me a form full of questions about my religious background. Many who transfer to Roman Catholicism from some other religious tradition go through a series of structured preparation classes and are then formally brought into the church during the Easter Vigil. Since I was a member of long standing in another liturgical church, whose more orthodox wing had always drawn me strongly, I decided that if I could answer honestly and specifically the set of questions asked, I would skip that process. Mysteriously, my well-founded disagreements with official Catholic policies seemed not to hold me back from "joining" the Basilica parish. My need was greater than my objections, so I simply answered the questions on the form and kept showing up in the pews.

Those questions presented no problem: I could say "yes" to belief in a creedal doctrine; I could provide dates for being confirmed and for receiving first communion. My promise to myself was simple: if anyone asked me if I had belonged to a specifically Roman Catholic church in the past, I'd say "no," and enroll in classes for adults from other faith systems seeking membership in the Catholic church. But if they accepted my answers and my steady participation, I would just merge my former knowledge, beliefs, and practices into the completely familiar rituals at my adopted church.

That was eight years ago, and no one has needed any further "proof" from me. Because I like to sit in essentially the same place every Sunday, even some obvious "old-timers" smile or nod or say "good morning." When I slide quietly into a pew and listen as the organist gives us one of his preludes, I sometimes flash back to being ten at Christ Church in Fairfield. I smile to myself as I realize I am duplicating my mother's behavior about having "her" pew, and I no longer attach elitist snobbery as her only motives. Like me, she may simply have found it reassuring to sit in the same place every Sunday. Certainly, on the rare occasions when I've had to sit elsewhere, the whole service has seemed slightly out of kilter. Why isn't my reliance on habit a sign of rigidity on my part? Since it doesn't seem that to me, perhaps my mother acted out of more complex motives that I originally assigned to her. In my own defense, I offer that my deep need for repetition stems from the comfort I find within it.

Chapter 6
This Pilgrim's Progress

*I*n the course of my life, I've made three spiritual journeys and two pilgrimages—twice to Assisi in Italy; once to Avila in Spain; once to Tanzania, in Africa, under the auspices of the Jane Goodall Institute; and finally to Iceland to commune with puffins. The word "pilgrim" means wanderer, stranger, traveler, but it has more specifically come to denote someone who travels far from home in order to visit places deemed sacred or special by the individual making the journey. A pilgrimage differs from a vacation in that the purpose is not to relax and play but rather to enter more seriously into some kind of geographical space where it is possible to transcend the self that usually consumes much too much of our energies. The idea of pilgrimages attracts me, so whenever I listen to someone who has "done" the sacred walk, for example the Camino de Santiago in Northern Spain, I yearn to try it, even making the last portion on my knees as the Christian pilgrim women once did.

When I was in college and first learned of the Stations of the Cross, I vowed someday to find a church that had old ones, probably in Paris or Rome, and "travel" from one to the other, contemplating what each moment might have meant in Jesus' life, and, more importantly, how I might translate the story in each image into my own life. Having joined a liberal Roman Catholic parish, I now am in such a setting in my own home town, but I have not taken advantage of the devotional practice of taking the Stations held during the Lenten season. Rather, I have a website that depicts the stations as designed by the woman who served as artist-in-residence at the Basilica for many years. Her idea of Christ is similar to that found in the major undertaking at nearby St. John's Abbey in Collegeville, Minnesota. In this project, which is resulting in a new illumination of the New Testament, an artist from England shows Jesus as a brilliant yellow vertical line. This turning away from specific incarnational representations pleases me, since my idea of God has become ever more amorphous and ever less humanoid. No longer does my concept of God have any gender or physiognomy. God is a force, a presence, something perceived but unseen and, indeed, unseeable.

For me, then, each of my spiritual journeys has been a concentrated experience of getting closer to that presence. Assisi, totally unplanned, captivated me when I was about nineteen. My mother had sent me on a tour of Europe sponsored by a highly reputable group in Birmingham. It was one of those whirlwind ventures in which one stays two days here and a day and a half there, riding around on large buses, gawking at famous statues and buildings, rushing through old churches or museums, and winding up with myriad snapshots and a few fragmented memories. But when the bus found its way on the narrow road leading to the center of Assisi, I felt something powerful. Amongst the faces of local residents, I expected to see Francis in his brown robe and sandals. Other priests and monks did appear, dressed in brown robes and sandals, so I invested them with some of his aura. So strong were these feelings that I woke myself up before dawn on the one full day we were to have in the town. Leaving my little pensione, I walked toward the highest visible building which was, of course, the tower and steeple of a church. Finding it open even in the day's first-light, I crept inside and heard monks chanting in the space empty of all but themselves. For years thereafter, I would tell people "I have found my spiritual home"—Assisi.

About twenty years ago, my partner and I decided to include the old city, which she had never seen, as part of an Italian vacation. Our hotel was within a few feet of a walled-in church space that had a tiny door that opened directly off the sidewalk. While she unpacked and tried to sleep before our first dinner, I set off to investigate what lingered in my memory so deeply. When I came upon the small door, I gave it a push and found myself inside a tiny chapel into which came almost at the same moment that I entered from the outside about fifteen nuns issuing from some inner sanctum and chanting in Latin. Quietly I slipped into a seat and sat mesmerized by the crystalline quality of their voices and the concentration of their devotion. Once again, I had seemed to have fallen into a deeply spiritual moment with no prior planning or expectation.

Because we had read that St. Francis himself had found Assisi too "busy" and "noisy," though it still had retained its small town flavor so many centuries and changes later, we hired a car and driver to take us to the monastery up above the city to which the saint often climbed in order to meditate and pray undisturbed. For the hour we spent on the grounds of that holy place, no other visitors appeared. We were led by an elderly nun whose joints seemed to ache as she moved deliberately, and who spoke no word of English to our speaking no words of Italian. She communicated, however, by using hand gestures and facial expressions. We sensed that she was showing us Francis' favorite wooded nook at one point and, as we turned a corner to see more of it, two stunningly white doves flew up from a bush and hovered near us before flying further into the woods. Their sudden appearance seemed an omen to my partner and me—we were sure they were the saint's spirit blessing us as we stood reverently amidst the blooming, light yellow hibiscus plants. Once again, I affirmed the intimate connection in my heart between flowers and spirituality.

At one point, the sister unlocked a heavy door and led us into a small room holding only an unadorned wooden altar with a large crucifix hanging above it. Through her excellent gesticulations, we understood that this was the final retreat for the man who kept feeling life around him as a distraction from union with his God. Francis kept freeing himself from earthly distractions so as to draw ever nearer to the God of his understanding.

We were in Assisi only shortly after a major earthquake had wreaked serious destruction to the cathedral named for their patron saint. Only parts were open, but we watched a moving video about the massive efforts to repair and reconstruct as much of the edifice as possible. The goal was to have the cathedral ready for a special visit at Easter by the Pope, so volunteers were working feverishly. A kindly priest with a good command of English told me that he and his fellow clergy had been dumbfounded at the outpouring of free help, coming equally from day laborers and company executives, all devastated by what had happened to their beloved church building. He spoke of this unexpected generosity of time and skills as a contemporary miracle, and I nodded agreement. Taking down an address to which cash contributions could be mailed, I was pleased to write a check upon my return home to help purchase materials and employ experts needed for the restoration. When the *New York Times* ran a short article on the back pages of the lead section of the paper, reporting on that visit by the Pope on Easter, I felt a tiny part of the reclamation effort as another outward and visible sign of what was surely a deeply felt inward and spiritual grace felt by all connected with restoring the cathedral.

My third journey in search of spiritual connection came about a decade after our time in Assisi. My partner and I decided to take a vacation in Spain, since neither of us had ever been to the country. We began by spending a week in Barcelona, being amazed by the playful yet powerful architectural feats, dispersed all over town, of Antoni Gaudi, and being a bit cowed by the active and loud street life of the metropolis. Since neither of us could speak or read Spanish, we really were tourists in the least positive sense of that word. We were not enjoying ourselves the way we always did in Paris where we had our favorite restaurant, church, park, and launderette. So, when I proposed a side trip to Avila, where surely it would be quieter and more to our liking, my partner agreed, having listened to my recital about St. Teresa's ecstatic visitations as recorded in her various writings. I hoped we might feel Teresa's spirit in the medieval, walled city, and that I could enjoy a special sense of closeness with a female saint who wrote so powerfully about her own experiences with God and Christ. So the side trip to Avila was made in anticipation but without genuine preparation.

St. Teresa is one of the most powerful mystics in western religious history. Living for much of the 16th century in Spain as a Carmelite nun, she founded seventeen convents and almost as many religious houses for males. She had visions that included one in which Jesus appeared to her in order to give her bread. The iconography surrounding her usually depicts her open hand receiving divine inspiration from a white dove or an angel placing his arrow or spear just where her heart would be under her flowing garments. She lived for over thirty years in a convent just outside the walled town of Avila. During the last few of these years, she was joined by St. John of the Cross, who served as her confessor.

Her mystical writings had excited me some twenty-five years before, when I was a graduate student in Nashville, full of religious fervor. I had felt close enough to Teresa to have contemplated joining a contemplative order myself. Life within the walls of such places, as portrayed by Teresa, seemed so simple, so regulated, so fulfilling. No worries about what to wear or when to get up or what to have for dinner. All that time to kneel in prayer or ponder the great silence that surrounds the godhead. For her own part, she favored what she called "mental prayer," defined by her as "taking time frequently to be alone with him who we know loves us," where that "him" was clearly Jesus. So she undoubtedly spent many hours in silent prayer, inside what she pictured as an "interior castle." One final connection I felt with her turns around her speaking about engaging in mystic prayer as being like "watering a garden."

In early March of 2003, then, we found the right train in the huge station and traveled the couple of hours to Avila. A friend had recommended we stay in one of the so-called paradors, old palaces turned into hotels for those who could pay the price of a room. Because this was a special occasion, I convinced my partner that we could spend the extra money. After unpacking in our four-star parador with its commodious rooms, we found ourselves in the smoke-filled downstairs lounge crowded with lots of heterosexuals drinking before dinner, which was not going even to begin until 8:30 p.m. Returning to our room to wait for the announcing gong, I complained about this European penchant for eating so late. With stomach growling and brain agitating, I kept hearing a strange clicking sound somewhere out our window, its source unknowable in the quickly fading daylight. Eventually I went outside to stroll the topiaried green garden just below our room. This process let me trace the origin of those sounds to a belfry forming part of the 13th c. wall that surrounds the entire town. Though it was already dusk, I could make out some kind of large bird on one of the ledges of the belfry. Tired from a long train ride and irritable at the long wait for dinner, which was delicious when it finally happened, I decided to delay making queries about the big bird until the next morning.

The bird turned out to be a stork, which then turned out to be one of scores of storks, all flying off from the ledges and steeples of every church and then returning with bits of straw for their nests. When they landed, they each clicked their beaks to greet a second stork whom I assumed to be their mate. These birds live in Avila spring, summer, and fall, only migrating elsewhere for the brief but too chilly winter. They had only recently returned for the new year and were busily making homes in preparation for stork babies. Having never seen a live stork, I was impressed by the magnitude of their bodies. They are huge fowls with wide wingspans, white except for black tips on each wing. Their feet and bills are bright red, and their clicking echoed throughout the town all day and into the night.

These storks were alive and engaged in the present and the future, while the town of Avila seemed distinctly frozen in the past. Tourists were much in evidence, eager to walk along the fortress wall, built between the eleventh and fourteenth centuries to protect the white Castilian residents from the "dark-skinned marauding" Moors who lived in the nearby mountains. Those Castilians reported on raids in which the barbaric hoards swooped down to capture the more "cultivated" Spanish. Pondering this culturally racist account of history, I flashed to Shakespeare's poignant tragedy, *Othello*, in which he shows so clearly the vulnerability of a noble Moorish captain who has little chance against the scheming hypocrisy of the Venetian Christians who exploit his military skills while scorning his dark skin.

Contrary to the storks who were busily planning for new life, the town seemed, except for the tourists, sad and abandoned. Many old buildings, uninhabited for who knows how long, were boarded up or crumbling into the street. Churches were empty, with no candles burning as they always have been when I have visited similar places in France and Italy. In fact, it was impossible to light a real candle anywhere in Avila. Each church had a little white box full of small cylinders in containers that were carefully covered by a sheet of thick plastic. If one deposited a coin of a certain denomination into a slot, one could then "touch" the plastic cover, and a tiny light bulb inside one of the cylinders would go on. Needless to say, I did not feel inclined to do that, nor did anyone else apparently, so all the churches we ducked into remained cold and dark. Streets seldom had many people walking in them, and those who did so looked harried or simply depressed.

Trying to "find" St. Teresa, we visited her convent. A young girl let us in—there was no one else visible on the premises—and closed us inside the convent walls, showing us the rope to pull that would ring a bell to alert her that we wanted to get out. Being alone in that setting could have been wonderful, but not in this instance. I felt vaguely imprisoned, not at all sure anyone would hear us and respond when we rang to be let out. A single sheet of paper told us what we were seeing, but there was no affect or aura left inside the place. Not even when we were looking at the visiting room in which Teresa "saw" Jesus did I sense her spirit. Spending far less time in this putatively sacred space than I'd imagined I would choose to do, we pulled the bell rope and waited what seemed too long to my anxious self for a different young person to free us. We left feeling disappointed and empty. This was not the pilgrimage I had hoped for, because the saint's spirit we sought had long ago departed the premises.

This experience stands in stark contrast with our time in Assisi when I had felt St. Francis everywhere. I felt his spirit inside "his" church, whose ceiling had recently collapsed during the massive and highly destructive earthquake. His presence could be felt on street corners where locals engaged in lively conversation, touching one another affectionately and often. Francis' aura was definitely lingering inside his retreat house a few miles out of town where that benevolent nun had taken us to see special places, and where those two white doves had flown up as we rounded a turn in our path, convincing both my partner and me that they were St. Francis' blessing.

I have thought often and deeply about what might account for the differences between Assisi and Avila. Both towns depend on tourists' interest in a person who lived in them a very long time ago, but the similarities seem to end there. It is certainly the case that Francis is widely known and invoked, even by non-practicing Catholics or people who have little truck with saints, while Teresa is more mystical and so less accessible to the general public. In Assisi, Francis and the past are loved; in Avila, Teresa and the past are preserved. Preservation has an embalming effect whereas the Italian's love for their patron saint adds life and vigor to what pervades Assisi, perched on its gently sloping hill. Most of Avila's residents have moved to the outskirts of the town, where they live in boring white-washed complexes from which they bus into their formerly enlivened streets and shops to serve the immediate needs of transient visitors. By spending time in these two historic towns that once housed spiritual giants, however, I learned an invaluable lesson about how to handle the past. I can reenter it through my senses, as is the case with Francis and Assisi. I can appreciate it rationally, as is the case with Teresa and Avila. But, even though Teresa's spirit seemed absent in those tourist-filled streets, the storks of Avila were utterly magical, providing a powerful linkage between me and a past that included the saint and her visions of Jesus. The storks redeemed our trip, and, by concentrating on the big birds, I salvaged a little of what was to have been a genuine pilgrimage. If Teresa has taken refuge from the tourists who enter her convent, perhaps she is mystically part of the yearly return and mating of the giant and graceful birds.

———

My third journey that really was a formal pilgrimage, undertaken in 2008, also seems the most significant to my present and future spiritual life. If one definition of a pilgrim is being a "stranger," then planning such a venture with one's beloved automatically softens that status. No matter how "foreign" or "strange" may be the surroundings or events that occur, the pilgrim has a familiar and soothing anchor in the company of that other person. While experiencing Assisi and Avila with my life partner had in no way lessened the impact of what I saw and felt, her very presence provided me with some kind of spiritual echo since our responses so often mirrored each other. So when I made the momentous decision to travel to Tanzania with a small group of strangers led by someone connected with the Jane Goodall Institute, I was opening up entirely different possibilities.

I had dreamt of going to Africa ever since I was in my early thirties and first read Isak Dinesen's highly romantic autobiographical work, *Out of Africa*. Watching Robert Redford and Meryl Streep in the stunning movie version of the book only reinforced my desire to stand on some of that hallowed ground. Upon retirement in 2001, after almost four decades in the English Department at the University of Minnesota, I asked friends who wanted to give me a gift to contribute to a trip to Kenya and Tanzania. Simultaneously, I asked my partner to accompany me on the trip, and she agreed, though with a degree of reluctance since she hated getting shots and was apprehensive about what might befall us. After signing up with a tour group for people over fifty-five and getting the long series of shots, we were stymied from leaving because terrorists bombed U.S. embassies in both of our destination countries and the State Department cautioned against all American travel.

In the years following this huge disappointment, I became involved with supporting the Goodall Institute's work to save the treasured chimpanzees in the Gombe Reserve in Tanzania. Because I'd made a significant donation, I'd even been able to meet Jane Goodall on one of her visits to Minnesota. In her presence, I had felt the tremendous power of her vision for her beloved and threatened primates. By continuing to donate a certain amount of money, I became part of a group who are offered each year a chance to go on safari and then to visit the chimpanzees in their native habitat. Each spring when the letter outlining this adventure arrived, my partner urged me to go, saying she honestly could not psyche herself up again to accompany me, but she would gladly care for our home, garden, and cats while I fulfilled such an old and powerful dream. Unwilling to embark on such a momentous undertaking without her, however, I kept refusing, giving most of what the trip would cost to support the Institute's on-going projects. Then, when my partner asked to end our relationship, I assumed I'd never get to Africa.

The spring after she moved out, the annual letter arrived in my mail box, and I read it again, thinking to recycle the paper as soon as I finished. Something stayed my hand, however, and I left it out on the kitchen counter where I'd see it every day. Tours have never appealed to me, but I figured no one would sign up for this one unless s/he were serious about the preservation of natural treasures, so I called the 800 number and spoke with the woman who would be the group's leader. After that long and reassuring conversation, I began to light a special candle at the Basilica, asking as I knelt on the small *prie dieu* facing the Madonna of Guadaloupe for help in making the best choice about Africa. Every Sunday, I begin my public worship time with a private devotional practice of lighting one of the three-day candles just inside the church. Often I put friends who are ill or grieving or facing difficult choices into the light of that candle. Always I ask that I may step out of my egocentric self enough to be open to what is about to happen in the communal service. My answer about going to Tanzania came the third week of placing my question into the candlelight: I was not getting any younger, so if I were ever going to realize my old wish to visit Africa, I needed to get on with it. Within a week of that message's reaching me, I had signed the application and sent it to the address in Virginia where the Goodall Institute is located.

When I began telling friends of my decision, they were excited about my "wonderful vacation." That didn't feel like the right word. When I told my grief counselor, whom I had been seeing since the dissolution of my long-term relationship, of the decision, her face lit up as she said "This doesn't seem like the usual vacation, right?" Relieved that someone comprehended the momentous nature of my decision, I eagerly agreed. When she pushed me to say what the trip was, if not a vacation, I heard myself say, "It's a pilgrimage." Immediately, my counselor recommended a book that she owned, written by Phil Cousineau and entitled *The Art of Pilgrimage*. Braving the world of Amazon.com, I ordered my own copy and began reading it slowly several months prior to departure.

The author is well-read in the literature written by men and women intent upon traveling to places where they might seek and find the very heart of life's mysteries. Such people are all pilgrims and I sincerely believed I could join their ranks in Tanzania. Cousineau's list of readings by such people swings from ancients like Epictetus to moderns like Muriel Ruykeyser and Van Morrison. Many of Cousineau's quoted passages emphasize that pilgrims walk in the steps of others similarly seeking life's secrets, and that true pilgrims focus always on the moment. As one such person, John Daido Loori, puts it, "If you miss the moment, you miss your life." Mr. Loori is an author, artist, and Zen master who founded the Zen Mountain Monastery in Mount Temper, New York, known for integrating various art forms into traditional Zen practice.

Cousineau believes that one cannot just step off an airplane in some distant locale and begin being a pilgrim, so he recommends "practicing" being a pilgrim in one's familiar surroundings before setting off on the main journey. So I began taking one of his recommendations with me on my solitary morning walks in my neighborhood, or in nearby parks or along urban lakes in Minneapolis. Over the several months of conscious preparation, I managed to practice most of Cousineau's major suggestions that included the following:

- Think of this as a transformative journey to a sacred center
- Keep a curious soul that goes beyond the boundaries
- Slow down to experience metamorphosis
- Beckon the darkness within me, as early pilgrims always did
- Listen/pray/look/ask
- See things for myself, keeping the intention of attention highly developed
- See all as portentous, especially the ordinary aspects of each day
- Stay mindful, asking what have I seen today, what have I felt
- Ponder the etymology of "thrill"—a vibration when the arrow hits its target.

The last thing I did, following my guide's recommendation, was to take along some kind of talisman. I quickly settled on a perfectly rounded pebble I'd picked up on the shores of Lake Superior decades before, probably in the 1970s when I spent long weekends at an old lodge on the Cascade River during spring break from the University of Minnesota where I taught. I asked people to hold the magic stone in their hands and put into it their wishes for me as I embarked upon this momentous journey. I ended up asking seventeen close friends and one special cousin to fill my little pebble with their words, words I recorded in the beautiful leather-bound, small journal I had found to accompany me on my quest. Some of their offerings were "God's peace," "joy," "lightness," "VROOMMM," "awe-struck," "comfort," "accomplishment," and "horizon." Feeling strongly protected and loved, I boarded the plane in Minneapolis that would take me to Amsterdam where I would find a second plane that flew into Dar es Salaam in Tanzania. I felt as ready for what lay ahead of me as it was possible to be.

What I wasn't and couldn't have been prepared for was what would happen to me once on the ground in Tanzania. We land briefly in Kilimanjaro. No view of the famous mountain, with or without its snows, because it's late at night. The airport terminal is charmingly small, like ours used to be when I first flew from Birmingham, Alabama, in the 1950s. The plane stops many feet from the terminal, out on the tarmac, and a set of old-fashioned metal steps is rolled up to the side door for use by those deplaning. Our steward leaves the doors open, and a light Tanzanian breeze blows into our cabin— humid but soft, not close or sticky like Minnesota humidity. A local crew, dressed in bright red and yellow uniforms set off by their coal black skins and handsome physiques, come aboard to clean the cabins. Talking animatedly and laughing with one another, they quickly and efficiently take away crumpled newspapers, squashed plastic cups, and big bags of trash. Finally, they run a tiny carpet sweeper down the center aisle, leaving us neat and tidy for the short hop from Kilimanjaro to Dar es Salaam.

After an overnight stay and breakfast in Dar, we fly in two small, chartered planes to the oldest game preserve in Africa, the Selous National Park, located in the eastern section of Tanzania. Our flight to it and the subsequent boat trip to our camp give me my first chance to put Cousineau's principle of "ask what I've seen today and how I've felt" into practice. Here is a partial accounting of that initial exposure:

- Thin clay-colored strips on the ground way below us, stretching sometimes for long distances, sometimes petering out after just a few yards, always located in the middle of vast and lush green plains. The longest ones almost fade at certain points, only to resurface quite red a little later. These eventually simply vanish amidst clusters of very small buildings I assume to be tribal dwellings. The pilot tells me the strips are ribbon roads, well-known to locals, barely distinguishable by visitors.

- Bright yellow, small birds with red heads darting in and out of the low-lying, dense bushes all along the Rufiji River. I see these from one of several little square-nosed boats we boarded at the airstrip to take us to our camp. Our naturalist, "Amazing" Augustine, as we dubbed our guide with his graduate degrees in ornithology and zoology, tells me they are golden weavers who love the bushes full of big red blossoms. They are called "weavers" because of the shape of their nests—beautiful, tightly woven baskets hanging gracefully from branches. He also tells us there are many varieties of weavers, one of which makes messy nests but is still afforded the honorific title.

- Very tall vertical objects rising suddenly and powerfully out of the Rufiji River. I take them to be ancient totems, vestigial statements about a former moment in time. When I ask Augustine about them later, he tells me they are dead palm trees, killed by uncommon floods that had swept through the region the past year, gradually suffocating the stately trees. So actually, they are testaments to the present moment in time, when climate change is being felt rather than debated. I think my noticing them, finding these sentinels powerful and beautiful, "counts" with Augustine who seems entirely pleased with my questions and responses.

Our tour leader kept telling us we were seeing things her previous groups had never seen or that experienced naturalists seldom saw. One such gift was coming upon a mother cheetah and four tiny cubs just far enough from our vehicle to keep us from disturbing them when we stopped to observe them more closely through binoculars. At first when I looked, all I could see was the mother and a lump of bright tan and black spots lying just above ground level. As I watched, however, the "lump" morphed into the four babies, all huddled together for warmth or protection or company or all of the above. Augustine broke into our "oohing" and "aahing" to tell us the hard fact that the mother would be lucky if she saw one of her babies reach adolescence. Male cheetahs have nothing to do with caring for the young once they have implanted their sperm, so the female must both forage for food and try to protect her young while doing so. Obviously, the babies are left dangerously vulnerable to hyenas, large birds, and foxes. The reason the ball of baby cheetahs was almost at ground level, then, was definitely for protection. The mother had dug out a shallow cup in the earth and piled her young into it, hoping thereby to make them less visible to prey. My own idea of God is very like that mother cheetah—my God works hard to protect me from harmful forces, often encouraging me to make myself small or insignificant so as to avoid the notice of predators of various sorts. And my God often offers the only shelter available as I move into a new phase of my life.

I had what I consider a visitation the second night we were at the Selous National Park. Getting only about three hours sleep the previous night, I turn off the light early, hoping to fall into a deep repose. No such luck, so I continue reading. I finally doze off about 1:00 a.m., only to awaken to distant rumblings of thunder. Within minutes it is raining and blowing, gently at first but rapidly whipping up quite a gale and downpour. My elegant tent house has lots of long white curtains that can be pulled across the screen walls at night, to make us less conspicuous to nocturnal animals foraging quite close by. As I lie listening to the rain on my bamboo roof, all four of these diaphanous white curtains across the back of my space facing the river begin to billow out softly. Within minutes, they are flapping harder and harder, lifting in the wind until they are fully horizontal. They become a mammoth cape or, better yet, giant wings reaching out to enfold me. At first, I feel apprehensive and consider getting up and pushing them aside so as to prevent this wild display. When I think of them as wings, however, I relax, comforted by their animation. For about half an hour, I lie quite still, listening to the storm and entering the mystical "place" created by the gauzy wings.

The rain continues in torrents for over an hour, punctuated by glorious lightning bursts out over the lake about thirty yards from my tent. I am filled with an overwhelming sense of God's peace and protection even as I marvel at the power of this moment when the universe seemed intent upon speaking to me. T.S. Eliot's long poem,

The Waste Land, came to mind, especially the last section entitled "What the Thunder Says." The last words are exactly what I heard in the storm: "shantih shantih shantih"—Sandscrit for "the peace that passeth understanding." When finally the curtains resumed their limp folds over my screened window, I emerged from the experience changed, more open to what lay ahead of me, more open to what stirred within my spirit.

For the rest of our first week, we witnessed amazing animals at Selous, on the Serengeti Plain, and finally, at the bottom of the giant Ngorongora Crater. Each day I felt immersed in something bigger and older than what we "moderns" have decided is civilization, marveling at lions catching baby impalas, or giraffes feeding from impossibly high branches of acacia trees. God seemed present in each new encounter in Tanzania, even as I seemed less and less important to what was happening around me. As a witness to the panorama I was seeing, however, I felt I was a tiny part of what is described with such beauty in the opening chapter of Genesis. These animals and the floral world they inhabit took on a kind of edenic innocence seldom seen by me as someone living in a big city and in a time when the natural world is in great danger from us humans.

One moment of witness to such primal innocence comes on an afternoon outing where I have chosen to ride with one of our excellent drivers rather than taking a long hike. Our driver, Allen, believes he can find a lion who has been spotted the previous day, so we head off on a mission. It feels good to be in Allen's vehicle because I've been impressed by all he knows about the flora and fauna, finding out later that he wants to start an educational program to become a naturalist like Augustine. Though I'm quite content on this drive to marvel at the groupings of giraffes, the stunning birds, a single golden baboon sitting quietly under a tree, in the afternoon shade, the scores of zebras eating and occasionally braying, and a large antelope called an eland, Allen keeps pushing further until the gift appears. He whispers "simba," as he turns off the engine. We've come upon a mother lion with her two cubs barely bigger than my beloved kitties, Minna and Sophie. Allen tells us they are four months old, that there were originally five in the litter but that three have been killed by other animals, so the mother is particularly vigilant about protecting the remaining two. By cutting his engine and rolling our vehicle along the deeply rutted roadway, Allen gets us within ten feet of the lions. He stops, and we all sit mesmerized by the tableau playing out before us. After about fifteen minutes, the mother moves off, calling gently to her cubs who follow immediately though not in a straight line. We lose sight of them behind a boulder, so I assume our experience is over. But Allen drives a few yards to a slightly wider place in the road, turns us around, and inches back to the boulder. Using the extra gear, especially designed by Toyota for more difficult terrain driving, he slowly descends around the big rock until we come upon the three nestled together, the mother licking her babies, one cub climbing up on her stomach only to slide back down into the grass landing on his or her backside. At one point the lion looks right at us—wise, a little tired from her efforts to keep her precious babies alive, utterly peaceful in her body and her space. My sense of awe is sharply broken by an unbidden thought: "How could anyone possibly pull a trigger and take that look away forever?"

The second week of my pilgrimage to Tanzania took us to villages along the route to Gombe, where Jane Goodall's precious chimps live. As our special safari vehicles drove slowly through each village, children lined the unpaved and deeply-rutted streets to wave at us and jump around happily. While the young children seemed genuinely excited to see us, teenagers ignored us, and many young adult males glared at us as they looked up from their outdoor pool tables where they were clearly playing for money. Since it was the middle of the morning or early afternoon as we drove along, these young men obviously had no regular jobs, so understandably they probably resented us with our leisurely and economically secure lives.

This second week was designed to show us some of the successful projects sponsored by the Goodall Institute in their efforts to win support from villagers in the urgent campaign to protect the forest environment without which the chimps simply cannot survive. One of these projects is located on a high plateau overlooking gorgeous Lake Tanganyika, Africa's deepest lake, extending many miles from North to South. A Tanzanian forestry expert tells us that only nine years earlier where we are standing was bare expanse. All trees had been logged for firewood or building material. So Jane Goodall herself visited the President and proposed the following: "Give us this denuded plateau, and we will bring it back by planting seedlings."

Since the tract was useless to the government, the President agreed, and the reforestation project began. After nine years, we found ourselves in a gorgeous, thickly wooded area, full of high grasses and small-to-medium sized trees. Our guide smiles broadly as he tells us that, because of the undergrowth and trees, small animal life is returning, e.g., squirrels, foxes, and ground snakes. His hope is that larger species will follow, making this new forest a sustainable habitat for various creatures being pushed out of other regions. I feel, as he speaks to us in such proud and loving terms, that I'm watching a small miracle unfold, not all at once like many performed by Jesus, but no less powerful for being slower and more dependent on human work.

Finally, the time comes to boat down Lake Tanganika to the climax of this pilgrimage, the chimpanzees of Gombe. Along the way, I am saddened to see some mountainsides completely denuded of their life-giving trees. They stand out because they are dark clay swatches amidst what should be unbroken greenness. The deforestation process causes creeping erosion of essential habitat. The beauty of the clear water and the charming sight of baboons running along the shoreline, as if to serve as harbingers of what awaits us, are marred by the reality of human encroachment.

When we land at the research center, we are greeted by a man named Jumanne whose history with Jane is long and deep. Taking us to a spot on the shoreline, he tells his story: "When I was seven years old, my father and the other fishermen of the village heard that 'a lady is coming to study the chimpanzees.' Most of the men became anxious and somewhat hostile since they feared that this 'lady' might see their fishing as harmful to the animals. When her little boat landed, and she climbed out with her mother, my father approached and offered to help unload their belongings. Unlike so many, my father was not afraid of the lady, so he went up close to her. Since my father went up close to her, I went up close to my father and helped carry things." This dear man, hardly as tall as I am, has lived his entire adult life helping Jane and her research teams. At one point, she paid for him to attend college where he got a master's degree. He now serves as the administrative head who welcomes each new scientist, helps him or her acclimate to the setting, and, importantly, mediates any problems that arise between or among the teams studying the chimpanzees and their surroundings.

As Jumanne spoke of Jane, he teared up. When I spoke to him at the end of his story, I teared up, seeing him as the human link to Jane, who is the human link to the primates, who are the equally human link to me. He has been close to her, and she has been close to the chimps; so my being connected to him, even briefly, strengthens my ties to her. The two of us clearly feel something intense happening between us. Jumanne wears a little white crocheted cap that I recognize as part of Muslim male attire. When I say, "Are you Muslim?" he lights up, proudly affirming my hunch. How little it takes from those of us with culturally different traditions to reach the hearts of people whose beliefs are not our own, just as Jumanne has reached mine. If this relative stranger and I can accomplish so much with so little effort, why can't high-level diplomats or political leaders do the same so that there is genuine appreciation of diversity? Never has this question seemed more pressing to me than as I stand on the shore of Lake Tanganika in Tanzania in Africa, engaged in deep conversation with someone who, in his wisdom, is entirely open to finding common ground.

February 18, 2008—the day I've been waiting for the whole time we've been here—we get to see, or try to see, Jane's beloved chimps. I have slept well over-night, which surprises me since often when I'm excited about what lies ahead, I sleep fitfully and wake early. What draws me out of slumber are forest sounds—birds mostly, and wind swaying large old trees to make a soughing sound that reminds me of northern Minnesota in the dead of winter. We spend four hours in that forest, climbing almost straight up, hearing chimp calls all around us. The research center tries hard to make as soft a footprint, literally in this case, as possible. The park guide, Abdulla, who leads us ever upward, is particularly solicitous towards me, causing me to believe that he's been told to help me see chimps if at all possible.

At what turns out to be a crucial moment, Abdulla draws me off from the trail as we scurry toward a group of trees in which he has spotted chimpanzees. It's a mother and her youngster, another mother with a tiny baby riding on her back, and several adolescents all swinging from tree to tree or pausing a few moments to eat something particularly tasty. Just as I've gotten my eyes completely in sync with this sub-group, Abdulla motions me to follow him quickly, and I do. He brings me below a single tree and points upward. There, right above me, no more than thirty feet, is a single largish chimp, sitting comfortably in the elbow of a big branch, happily chewing something pale green and pendulous. Abdulla tells everyone else to go on, that he'll stay with me. The gift of that action is fifteen minutes in which I am absolutely alone with the chimp. Abdulla has discreetly withdrawn so that I may have this magical experience. I feel a little like a primatologist myself as I sit utterly still, watching in total silence as the chimpanzee continues munching. At intervals, released strands drift down, one falling right into my lap. The tendril is sticky and I assume it has given the animal something sweet, the way honeysuckle blossoms gave me tiny squirts of sugary liquid when I was a child plucking the pale yellow blooms to suck dry. I handle these strands because they seem to take me closer to the animal I've flown half way around the world to see. Finally, the chimpanzee is done with his meal and moves lithely off to another tree. I get up, stiff from my stint of frozen animation but utterly connected to my Old World relative. Noting the end of the tableau, Abdulla silently reappears and motions me to follow him as we begin our descent to the lake shore where we join the others.

Sometimes, on a morning in Minneapolis when I've slept badly the preceding night, I think about not getting up in time to make my aerobics or stretch class at the local YWCA. But, by working my aging body hard, I realized a dream in Tanzania that was denied to several of the members of our group unable to complete the trek. Bodies fail, challenges daunt us, but I believe that keeping to my regimen of exercise and healthy diet paid off in this crucial moment. So my reflections at the end of that magical day in Gombe centered around the intimate connection between my daily choices about diet and exercise, and my ability to seek and find God in difficult places.

In my continuing search for that God, I think about and plan other prospective pilgrim journeys: Plitvice Lakes National Park in Croatia, known to natives as "Land of the Falling Lakes"; our own Grand Canyon that I have never seen except in photographs; Bear River Migratory Bird Refuge in Salt Lake City, written about so powerfully by Terry Tempest Williams in her memoir, *Refuge*. These

dream destinations have as their locus natural settings where humans
are secondary and other creatures and creations take precedence,
where I can shrink as I meld into or witness life and time outside my
puny span and compass. But I also become ever more convinced that
Dr. Samuel Johnson was correct when he has his restless protagonist,
Rasselas, learn that happiness and meaning may well reside right
outside our doors. So I also find my God at my backyard birdfeeder
as I watch three or four cardinal couples having their dusk snack or
on the crystal reflections off the water of Lake Calhoun just three
blocks from my house, or sitting in my pew at church as the choir
brings chills up my spine as they render some gorgeous Latin sacred
song or lead us in a familiar favorite hymn. In these kinds of small
and domestic settings, I am the same size as the rest of my world but
objects and moments suddenly take on wider significance because I
feel them suffused by the holy spirit of a being or force that is finally
unnamable but potent in my life.

———

My ideas about God and Jesus obviously have evolved over
the seven decades I've been alive. As I currently begin culling the
mountains of paper accumulated as an academic and a word-hound,
I keep coming across old letters or scribblings that let me glimpse
back to former moments when my attention focused on questions
of who and what God might be. On Easter Sunday of either 1959
or 1960, when I was either twenty-two or twenty-three, trying to
survive teaching at All Saints' in Mississippi, I wrote my mother a
long letter in which I explored my current stance on questions of
divinity. I quote it here in its entirety because it belongs in this work
written half a century later.

> In the 20th c. the various responses to religion range from
> complete rejection and scorn through honest questioning to
> frightened acceptance and mediocre allegiance. No one of
> these is good as an end and only the questioning is legitimate
> as a reasoned pattern. The man to whom we sing and pray
> on this day was neither a brutish aggressor nor a wimpy
> pacifist. He was a man in the full glory and beauty possible

to this form—a man who endured all the temptations and pain of humans in order to further understand us. He was a man who, finally, was willing to sacrifice his physical being on a cross of prejudice and then die from nails of fear and cruelty so that we might hope for more than a return to dust when life expired. This last gift proves that he was also God, for mere man could not have given this to a world of insensitive, hardened mockers.

If Christ were only man, the sheer drama of the crucifixion would be sufficient to move men [sic] for 2000 years, since we are sentimental enough to weep at the thought of piercing nails and stinging vinegar. But Christ is also God, and this we testify to each Sunday and certainly on this day, for no "mere drama" could concern itself with rising from physical death to spiritual life. In human "plays," we are limited by the very definitions of time and space. But God cannot be limited or He ceases to be God—therefore something as mysterious and awful (in the real sense of that word) as an empty tomb could only be another "act" in the realm of God's creation.

Through time, philosophers have offered elaborate proofs either for the existence or non-existence of God. I offer the above as not a proof but as a reason to believe. It isn't founded on fear or blindness or mediocrity. Christianity is not something easily understood and if we serve it "with water" to make it more palatable, then we deny both the Man and the God joined in Christ. We dilute to supposedly "protect"—the irony is that often the dilution destroys the essence and there is nothing to help or hurt the recipient. As we grow in age and grace, we must never be afraid to question the very heart of our beliefs and the beliefs of our heart.

This letter is full of earnest intellectual efforts to define what it means to me to say I am an Episcopalian. At the time of sending this missive, I was struggling to stay sane and employed in Vicksburg, so this exercise may have brought me temporary calm. If my mother responded, I have no recollection or surviving letter to indicate how.

I suspect she was simply a reliable sounding board who would not dismiss my elaborate arguments or think me foolish for trying to frame them. But the moorings of her faith were much simpler: she believed because she needed to. She did not worry about dogma or theological niceties since the solace her church gave her asked of her only attendance and service, both of which she was glad to give.

Now I am in my seventies—older than my mother was when she died—and, quite frankly, this old letter to her amuses me as it labors to find a "reason" to believe in Jesus' great love and in his sacrifice of life and breath. If asked to define my faith today, I would not weave such an elaborate pattern as this one. Rather, I'd remember the valuable model my mother offered me. I no longer let dogmatic disagreements keep me from gaining the spiritual sustenance that comes from believing without tangible proof. After all, there is no real need for faith if we have tangible proof. Today, I'd not write abstractly about what the incarnate God, Jesus, experienced as he lived and died. If I wanted to define God, I would probably talk about a great wall of plunging water at Niagara Falls, or miles of wildebeests trekking across the horizon in their yearly migration to Kenya when the feeding and watering begins to wane in Tanzania where they have given birth to a whole new generation of physically enigmatic creatures. But if I wanted to talk about Jesus, I'd talk about the miracle of perennials that reappear spring after spring in my garden—bleeding hearts with their Christian mythology, or tiny blue flowers that the birds spread in ever wider areas of my front yard. Or I'd think about how the poor and homeless people who knock on the side door of my church and are given, without any questions or identification, a sandwich and a cup of coffee. I try to emulate Jesus in my daily life, remembering what he was willing to do in order to honor his relationship to the God of his understanding and in order to provide me with a model.

Chapter 7
Lectio Divina

*T*hese days I am on the lookout for any practice that may deepen my conscious contact with my higher power. In 2009, the Basilica offered a Saturday workshop on something called *lectio divina*. Because it promised writing exercises—I was not writing since my personal life had been in too much upheaval—I decided to enroll, though I routinely shun such adult learning events.

About eight of us listened as a very smart retired priest told us the history of this spiritual discipline. Begun in the sixth century by Benedict and still practiced by Benedictines, *lectio divina* is a flexible practice, holding the distinction of being the oldest tradition within the Roman Catholic Church. We were told that it is not primarily an intellectual exercise, but rather spiritual and emotional. This is not "Bible study" for the purpose of "figuring out" what a given scripture might "mean." It is rather a practice intended to deepen one's prayer life by exploring how and where certain scriptural passages speak to us.

As I was taking notes from our facilitator, I flashed to a month in the late 1970s when I was in New York City on a research mission. The 42nd Street Public Library had, in its archives, many letters between May Sarton and Louise Bogan, 20th century American poets who were intimate friends for years. I wanted to read their correspondence in order to write an article about how women writers "networked" before there was an active second wave of the feminist movement. A friend had opened her apartment to me, and each morning, I arose early from my pull-out sofa bed, fixed strong tea and toast, and read from my AA books. I'd only been sober for a few years and found it helpful to begin each day by reading quietly. As mentioned earlier in this memoir, I decided to write responses in my journal to each day's brief reading, thereby prolonging my time spent reminding myself that I was a recovering alcoholic who intended not to drink that day. Sometimes I only wrote for a few minutes, but some days the words in the little blue book so spoke to my heart that I went on and on, creating pages of reflections that seemed quite similar to what our helpful group leader was asking us to do with Bible verses.

His schema for developing a *lectio divina* practice went like this:

- It is important to be relaxed before starting the readings, so we are to find a quiet place and engage in slow, deep breathing for a few minutes before taking up our Bibles.
- Only read a short portion of scripture. He told us psalms proved most evocative, so we would do well to start there. To be specifically helpful, he recommended we begin with psalm 139 since it stresses God's great love for us.
- Read each passage two times, making the second reading slower than the first and reading it out loud so we can *hear* the words and not just scan them.
- Sit quietly with the words, not taking up our writing exercise for some time. This part of the practice is to determine in what ways the words resonate.
- Say aloud and then write down specific words in the passage that call to us more than the rest.
- Write without thinking about form or diction, focusing on what those particular words make me think and feel.

- If the section of the psalm we first chose to read doesn't call to us, move on until we come to a section that does so. Then stay with that section for a longer than shorter period of time, letting ourselves sink further into our feelings awakened by the language.

Our facilitator stressed that *lectio divina* was about the spirit's movement within us, not about an intellectual understanding of scripture, so if we found ourselves retreating into our heads, we were to stop, breathe deeply a few times, and then see if we could return to a feeling level. We were to write about those words that "called out" to us, as our facilitator put it. When I taught poetry to undergraduates, I always asked them to read down the lines until a word or phrase stopped them. They were to use that moment as the entry point into the whole poem, working forward and backward from it to find out what the poem was saying to them. Clearly the practice of *lectio divina* was something I could embrace without difficulty.

Because some of what I wrote in the month or so after that workshop speaks directly to the direction my faith is taking at this stage of my life, I want to include a few examples. The first comes from reading part of Psalm 139: "Thou understandest my thought afar off." "Afar off" is what caught my emotional attention, and I quickly wrote the following:

> *As an orphan and now that I do not even have a sister, it seems as if most who have known me are "afar off" and so if I'm to understand them or feel them knowing me, it must be from a distance. Also I am recently without my life partner of 27 years, someone with whom I conversed often and closely on a daily basis for all those years. Much of our relationship was based on verbal delight in one another and in respect for what the other thought. We also valued highly what the other thought of us and so worked to be "known" as fully as we could be. Now she is also "afar off" though she lives only a few minutes from what was our home.*
>
> *If God knows me even though from afar off, how much*

more might I feel in touch with my Higher Power if I could find a way to lessen that distance. Would I feel less "alone" if I got in closer meditative contact with people from my past (or present) who are not in daily contact with me? The point is, and this is part of my deep grieving, NO ONE is in daily contact with me except my two kitties, Minna and Sophie, and we don't speak the same language. Being with them is like being with dear loving souls who speak Catalan or Urdu. I know of their love and caring and good dependence on me; they know, I hope, how much I love them through my behaviors and verbal contact. Maybe they could represent to me how it might be to be closer to God, who also doesn't speak "my" language. As a child and an adolescent, I decided that things would go better if I withheld much of what went on inside me. So I held back—I was the one afar off—for preservation purposes. Now I do not want to make myself partially invisible. I want the God of my understanding to see me and know me.

Another free-associational writing about Psalm 139 turns around the phrase "If I make my bed in hell, behold, thou art there."

There is no place where God is not to be found, even in the worst locations or states we put ourselves into. I am "found" by my Higher Power no matter where I go or what I do to avoid that source of loving support. This part of the psalm is all about being cared for and not alone, no matter how high or low we are in our lives. But do I believe this? Do I feel my God's presence at all moments and in all places? Was my Higher Power with me when I was drinking myself into oblivion or eating to such excess that I was in a perpetual fog? Well, something must have been there beside me or I'd never have stopped doing these self-destructive things. These words also argue for a non-specific "location" as the "home" of God, and that appeals to me. Devout Jews talk to and get angry at their God as if God were a "buddy" who was walking with them. There are stories of people who

*feel Jesus on the roadway beside them and who even report
seeing footprints to prove this.*

*I would like to be more in touch with that Higher Power
that loves and cares for me. It comes in tiny moments now,
but I hope to increase my contact, letting it become more
present in my daily routine. I'd like to have time many
mornings to sit and ponder these biblical words and then to
write words of my own in response to the readings. Often,
however, I feel suspended, looking at my own life and
retreating into an inert if focused watching and taking in
of other people's words through reading or watching good
DVD's from Netflix or my own tape library. I want my
God to be with me wherever I try to run and hide from
that source and from myself. The psalm says God will lay a
hand on me even if I fly way off into the sky or dive deep
down into the sea—distractions can't hide me from that
all-seeing, all-knowing power. So what is my obligation in
return? To be awake and aware, open to what that "hand"
conveys to me as it lies gently but steadily on my shoulder or
in my heart or in my mind.*

A final writing stemming from my slow readings of Psalm 139
takes off from the words, "They are more in number than the sand."

*This is said about God's thoughts to establish how infinite
they are. But I am watching the Planet Earth series, and
in the segment about deserts, Richard Attenborough shows
many thin spikes of things that once were huge mountains
but have been worn by wind and time into SAND,
forming deserts. So God's thoughts are like a desert in
relation to other geographical sites—vast and unbroken
and innumerable and unfathomable. So no wonder
Niagara Falls seemed to me to be "god" when my partner
and I visited it. It was vast, and the amount of water
was unfathomable. So when I am in Tanzania next year,
looking for spiritual renewal, I am apt to find it in settings
that are teeming with something or in vistas unbounded
by space and so by time, since time needs space in order*

to function and maintain itself. Timelessness, which is very like "god," depends, then, on an absence of objects or boundaries in space, on wilderness. God cannot, then, be "placed" somewhere since that limits the force that the term signifies to me. In the psalm, the poet is awed but also comforted by the fact that his God's thoughts are "more in number than the sand," so he too takes solace in vastness. I think of the Desert Fathers or of Moses or of Jesus in the desert for 30 days, finding God in himself and as himself. He needed to get away from cities and crowds and temples in order to do this. So people "wired" all the time may never find deep spirituality because they are in cramped quarters full of TIME measured not just in hours or minutes or even seconds, but in tiny tiny bits--nanoseconds. It's all reductive and that must depress God deeply.

The second psalm I chose was # 91, my all-time favorite from early childhood, probably because it promises that God will keep me from being hurt. In the intervening decades, I have surely been hurt often and deeply, yet I continue to be drawn to this psalm. Making it the focus of my new *lectio divina* practice seemed one way to explore that paradox. Since the words are so familiar to me, it took a while for any of them to jump out anew. The first to do so were these: "he shall cover thee with his feathers, and under his wings shalt thou trust." About them I wrote:

The image is of a mother bird/hen, drawing her little ones back to her protection. That protection is soft and warm and dark. It is quite different from other parts of this wonderful psalm where words like "fortress," "shield," and "buckler" suggest a more militant defense against one's trials. So is the psalmist suggesting a dual-gendered god, one who can be gentle and nurturing as well as warrior-like in the face of attacks? Am I to recognize that sometimes what I need from a higher power is help shielding myself from harms that confront me, and then sometimes what I need is just to be held and hidden away, not having to "fight" or defend myself, but simply needing to withdraw into a nest-

> *like place of feathers and wings. I like God as a huge bird, and so did Milton who figures God as "brooding" over the chaos of the deep in order to create the world.*

Once I started responding, it was as if every other phrase spoke to my immediate condition. Words flowed for several mornings and I felt truly revived in a simple faith that the God I pray to wishes me well and supports any efforts or choices of mine to achieve harmony in my daily life and peace within my soul. So my next focus was on the simple assertion, "thou shalt not be afraid...."

> *Here the promise is that nothing bad can come "nigh thee" because the listener has made God her habitation. What might it mean to make God one's "habitation"? A habitation is a place of dwelling, so it suggests that if someone could live under the "roof" of a higher power, that could protect one from pestilence at night and destruction at noonday. I remember as a young person feeling so safe when my mother read me these verses or, later, when I read them out loud or silently to myself. Do I still feel this level of protection? Certainly not literally, since our world is such that I could be attacked or injured or killed at any moment. But on some less literal level, I think I do feel shielded or at least accompanied through trials and sorrows.*

I begin to think this ninety-first psalm will remain at the center of my faith because I recall its comforting verses whenever I feel frightened or existentially alone.

Especially in the years since my long-term partner ended our relationship, I have felt some of its key phrases emerge from my grieving state to allow me space to imagine a bearable present and a safer future for myself. When I took my devastating news to a 12-step sponsor, one of her first comments was, "God would not have asked you to bear this burden so late in your life unless there were something you are to learn and do as a result of facing it." At the time she said this, I was very far from being able to agree, but promised to write it down and look at it periodically. It's now eight years later, and I do get glimmers occasionally of what that "something" might turn out to be. I even imagine that undertaking this spiritual memoir is part of what the God of my understanding has in mind for me. I am using what talents I have for writing to enter a previously unarticulated part of my life. That can't be a bad thing, surely—not to the power figured by David in so many of his beautiful poems.

Psalm 1 was the psalm my father once told me was his favorite. It's one of the shortest and is all about the righteous "man" who doesn't associate with any bad people or do bad things or even think bad thoughts. At one point the psalm reads, "he shall be like a tree planted by the rivers of water." What a lovely image of a tree by a river where it will be nourished easily. The psalm goes on to talk about leaves staying in season and about the tree/man having good fortune follow it/him. Did my father long for this kind of nirvana? Certainly his life was not like that at all. And where would my father have come upon such ease? His father was an alcoholic traveling salesman who left his wife and three children to fend for themselves while he went around planting peach trees and being with other women, and, of course, drinking. He also fished a lot. He was rather like the lilies of the field, neither sowing nor reaping really, since dropping peach seeds into ground is not exactly farming. So I could feel sad and sorry for my father if this psalm suggested something to him about a world so far from the one life had afforded him.

These days, as we dry out the world by abusing natural resources and warming of the globe, I feel sorry for the trees that are in such distress this summer in Minneapolis because of our deep drought. I must remember to trickle the maple on my boulevard this morning after I water with the hose. It hurts my heart to see what humans are doing to the earth. It would hurt David's heart, surely, since his psalms are full of images of the natural world as a reflection of God.

My notes from my *lectio divina* exercises show that several other passages from Psalm 1 resonated for me. The next seems to be this verse: "Like the chaff which the wind driveth away." About it I wrote,

> *This refers to the "ungodly" who are cast out in these last verses of this psalm that is all about separating sheep from goats, promising sheep sustenance and protection while*

goats get abandoned and derided. Did my father adhere to a more Old than New Testament version of reality? Did he wish someone had or would punish his ne'er-do-well father who left his family? Did he fantasize about powerful separators because he had very little control over his own life most of the time? Whatever the answers to these questions, the reason the phrase sticks with me is the vast gap between the force of the wind and the ability of little wisps of grain to withstand it. My present sense of what happens to the "ungodly" if they are Americans is quite different from this, i.e. , such people often are NOT driven out or excluded from THIS world. And we the people are too often like "chaff" in that we refuse to exercise even the power we do have to withstand the assault from the truly ungodly persons who wield power. It also interests me that the very first of David's psalms, the FRAME if you will, is all about judgment and NOT about love which figures in so many of the later pieces.

My mother's favorite psalm was # 101, also quite short, but, unlike my father's, full of love and joy and SONG.. The phrase "serve the lord with gladness and come before his presence with singing" prompts this entry:

My mother loved to sing and was so sad over my sister's total lack of talent; I wasn't must better, but at least I tried to sing hymns at church, just as I continue to do today. This psalm talks about how it is God who made us and not we ourselves—humility, something I saw in Mamie despite her self-centeredness. The part she liked best was about entering into the Lord's "gates with thanksgiving and into his courts with praise." That's more about joyfulness and paying glad homage, not fearful-about-judgment obedience. This is a view of a higher power that suits me nicely except when I get down on myself or others for not measuring up. I wonder if my mother was forgiving, more so than my father. If so, surely the fact that his father walked out on his young family enters into his leaning toward punishment of the unrighteous. His college career was aborted by that walk out; he had to go to work much too soon. So maybe feeling righteous helped him bear what he lost. There's a wonderful picture of my father in his football uniform as a college freshman, outdoors, standing with legs spread wide and hands on his waist, full of energy and pride. That person is someone lost to me entirely, since the father I knew worked at a desk during the day and read the newspaper or popular magazines at night. The only time he "played" was the week we spent every summer in Fort Walton, Florida, when he went out crabbing at dawn at least once, usually twice. My mother, on the other hand, seemed happier with her lot. She spent more than he earned but it kept her excited over new pretties for the house or her person. She had good bonds outside the home in her garden club and the church and then, once Daddy died, as a substitute teacher in the local grammar school where she adored the children and they her. My mother needed a bigger arena than home and family. But this psalm tells me something deep about her— she could feel joie de vivre and a clear love of music and of celebration.

I fell away from the daily practice of *lectio divina*, even though doing it brought me close to my love of metaphor as well as my sense of spiritual alertness. If I try to name why I did this, I come up against an old fact about myself: I shy away from pursuing certain aspects of my life because there is some shadowy but potent reluctance to be as good at some things as I could be were I to give them sufficient focus and repetition. In the early days of the second wave of feminism in the 1970s and 80s, a brother-sister pair published a book about women and men studied in relationship to how they made important career decisions. They determined that women held themselves back from key opportunities because, fearing failure, they opted not to try at all. Their argument felt all wrong to me, since I and so many women were entirely familiar with failure, even comfortable with it in some twisted way. What it seemed to me we feared was success. If we were truly successful at something, then we'd have to make whatever adjustments and sacrifices necessary to keep doing it. That was what frightened and at times paralyzed us.

Throughout my adult life, I have encountered just such fears and usually have chosen not to step further into whatever it was I was good at. In my late teens, I was told I might have sufficient talent to become a concert pianist. I chose not to devote myself to the requisite discipline centering around hours of practice and involving a diminished personal life. At one point in my life, I wrote several better than average poems but wasn't able or willing to go far enough inside my own interior castle to find more of them.

Maybe I stopped sitting with a psalm each morning after breakfast, finding what spoke to me particularly, because the "success" I fear in doing so has nothing to do with external accomplishment or recognition. Were I to stay with *lectio divina*, I would eventually find my deepest feelings about God and Jesus and my relationship to these entities. Then I feel quite sure I would have to alter certain aspects of my life, and it is the fear of what that might entail that helps me stop short. Contrary to stopping playing the piano completely or stopping trying to write poems at all, my embrace of spiritual practices in the past eight years may signal an ability or at least yearning to find a middle. So, while I stopped sitting with the psalter and my journal every morning, shortly after I gave that up, I heard my self speaking to no one visible about wanting to write about faith. The result of that eerie sentence is this memoir, something I have stayed with for slightly more than three years, even though there have been days when all my default buttons or impulses have been to stop. "This has been important just as therapy for me at this turning in my life journey." "Who would want to read these ramblings, anyway?" "Converting this draft into something worth trying to find a publisher for will demand more energy and commitment than I can muster." These and similar sobriquets have floated through my mind many times, but I've kept plugging away.

The one exception to this pattern of stopping short of my real capacities has been classroom teaching, a skill and talent I undeniably have. Instead of being satisfied to be a "good" teacher, I have worked at improving constantly, even now after ten years of retirement from formal teaching. Perhaps I have been able to embrace this part of my talent set because it is something women are "supposed" to be good at, even though I insisted on working in a part of the academic world fiercely guarded by male members for several of the decades I taught at the University of Minnesota. Even at the height of my alcoholic drinking, I never missed a day of work, and students brought me not only their questions about William Shakespeare or Adrienne Rich, but their dilemmas about whether to flee the draft by going to Canada or whether just to go to medical school as their parents wanted or insist on following their own star that told them to work in the arts. Even though I was unable to get along with most of my colleagues because of their hostility and my own counter-productive behaviors, and unable to foster or maintain a life of scholarly writing until midway in my career, I reveled in what I could facilitate happening inside my own classrooms. And, even when I was hung over, watching young people "see" why Hamlet doesn't kill Claudius immediately, or how Tennyson can make us weep for Tithonus who asked for immortality without asking not to continue aging, or what Audre Lorde really means by asserting that there might be a black unicorn at the heart of white mythology thrills me.

Chapter 8
High Holidays

*I*n my youth, Advent meant that I got a pretty colored calendar with little windows that I opened from December 1st to Christmas Eve. As for Christmas itself, it signaled presents that, once opened, had to be displayed on my made-up bed every day for a week. My Episcopal church numbered relatively few children in its congregation, so there was no pageant. At school, we made Santas and peppermint canes to paste on the blackboard. At home, we had the usual tree, adorned with special ornaments shaped like teapots, animals, and well-lighted houses. These treasures stayed in boxes in our basement most of the year and were part of my mother's idealized time in Selma, Alabama, as a child. In addition to the usual strings of colored lights, we placed special bulbs, a few of which I still have though they stopped working many years ago. These vestiges include a fat Santa Claus, a lovely red bird, a little gnome-like figure wearing a pointed hat, and a house painted with windows showing people inside decorating a Christmas tree. For years I begged for tinsel, an item seen by Mamie as being too "new" for her taste. Eventually she gave in, and I was allowed to "throw" strands of the shiny material up into the upper branches of our long-leaf pine tree.

Clearly the birth of Christ was marked in my childhood world in distinctly ordinary ways. My mother and I (and very occasionally my father) did attend church on Christmas day, but I have no memories of anything special's having taken place. Since returning to formal services at the Basilica, however, Advent and Christmas have taken on far more significance. I now understand that the point of Advent is that we are waiting for the birth of the Messiah. Each of the Sundays begins with our singing the hymn "Take comfort my people," and goes on to affirm that at the end of our waiting, Jesus will be born to save us. While we are singing this to one tune, a solo violinist plays a refrain from "Oh come, oh come, Emmanuel," setting up a strain of melancholy longing for that birth. We are also told every Sunday that the overall message of the month before Jesus' birth is "God is with us," the literal translation of Emmanuel. This further reinforces our yearning to be joined with an invisible God through celebrating the corporeal miracle that is the birth of Jesus, the moment that will be celebrated during the Christmas midnight mass observance.

Lent, on the other hand, always had a more serious tone attached to it. A week before it began, my Sunday school teacher handed out little square cardboard objects called mite boxes. These were blue and white, with pictures of African and Asian children ranged around their four sides and a slot in the top for putting in one's coins. It was explained to us children that coins we put into our mite boxes would eventually go to help "little heathen children" across the globe, so we were to share our allowances with these tiny unfortunates who had not been "saved." (The word for this little box may well have come from the Biblical story of the widow who gave all she had and was much praised for her generosity. Her gift is named the "widow's mite" in the Bible story.) We were also encouraged to ask our parents and even near neighbors if we might not do special chores and earn a little extra that, again, was to be inserted into the slots. On Easter Sunday, before we were excused to go to our classes while our parents listened to the sermon, we marched up to the altar rail and handed in our boxes that were supposed to be full of jingling coins. My allowance was minuscule, so I grumbled about having to share it with people I didn't know or care about beyond some abstracted concerns for their "souls." And my mother forbade me from bothering neighbors with requests to earn money. She did let me take on the occasional extra task—dusting shelves that we didn't already dust every week or weeding a back bed that some times didn't get tended to as Mamie rushed to plant and prune and fertilize more conspicuous spots. But my mite box was never full, causing me momentary guilt when our teacher asked us how many had stuffed their boxes so full that not another single nickel or dime could be made to fit.

Lent also meant Mamie enlisted my participation in "giving up" sweets, something she pledged to do every spring, only to stop by the end of the second of the six weeks involved. My fidelity to her regimen lasted even less time than her own since I sneaked candy into my diet by ducking into the little store on the way to junior high school and using some of that meager allowance to get one or two Tootsie rolls or a chocolate sucker. No one, at home or church, ever saw fit to discuss with us children why we might want to give money or cut back consumption of sugar, and certainly no one spoke about the relationship of such behavior to our trying to comprehend what the man Jesus was enduring for the forty days before he would be nailed up on a cross.

At some point in my early adulthood, a minister suggested from his pulpit that we might consider what the Virgin Mary might be going through in her last month of pregnancy. This was such a novelty, I was shocked to remember that she really was pregnant and not just ecstatic about what an angel with his lily told her was a special blessing from God. So I meditated seriously about how Mary, not to mention her husband Joseph, might be feeling as this mysterious spawning was coming to fruition. Similarly, I can remember quite clearly the Sunday when Henry Hancock, the eloquent and detached Welsh Dean of St. Mark's Cathedral in Minneapolis, invited his congregation to follow his example and ADD something during Lent. He talked about our perhaps reading and studying one of the Gospels during this period, as he did, so that we could become more conscious about the life and impending death of our Lord. Because I so respected him and because his suggestion was entirely original in my history of failed attempts to give up this or that substance,

I undertook a similar regimen. I picked Luke's gospel and actually experienced a deepening appreciation for what happened to Jesus at the hands of those who pretended to believe in him. More moved by Peter's inability to stay awake than by Pilate's cowardice, I concentrated on betrayal by someone close as one of life's hardest psychological or emotional blows. I also thought of Shakespeare's fear of mobs in plays like *Julius Caesar*, where men who were quite rational in themselves could become deranged when caught up in a crazed crowd. So the people of Jerusalem could throw down palms before Jesus' donkey on Sunday and then execute the same person in a brutally cruel manner just five short days later.

Having traveled the painful path of leaving a church I had loved for decades and then having found a new spiritual community, I find that Lent has become a time of deep reflection. For those forty days, I stay home as much as possible and let myself feel whatever I feel, much of the time having little or nothing to do with Christ's drama. My theory is simple: Jesus repeatedly asks his apostles to be mindful, not to act impetuously, and to try to know themselves more fully. So any honest emotion can contribute to my current spiritual development because it increases my understanding of who I am and what I believe.

During the forty-days of Lent, I concentrate on what it might have been like to be facing certain betrayal and death, letting myself remember moments in my own life when some person or institution has behaved in such a way as to prompt me to feel betrayed. In addition, I read the psalms regularly because they declare the Lord's protection of those who love him and praise his name, even as they also affirm the goodness of the world created by a force outside of and far more powerful than ourselves. If much of the forty days of Lent are spent, then, in quiet contemplation, the days just before Easter are entirely focused on the events leading up to and including Jesus' trial, crucifixion, death, burial, and resurrection. At the Basilica, I have learned to call this period the Triduum, that period beginning Thursday evening and extending until Easter Day evening.

These days are among the highest and holiest of the church's liturgical year. On Thursday evening, we gather to listen to readings, celebrate mass, strip the altar until Easter, and—the climax of the evening for me—wash one another's feet if we choose. Having its origin in the Gospels, this practice mirrors Jesus' washing the feet of his disciples to model service to one's fellow beings. At the Basilica, wooden stools are brought out and lined up in front of the altar. Additionally, there is water in pitchers along with basins to catch water poured over individual feet. People wishing to participate go up to a stool, sit down, and have their feet washed by the person who has just had her or his feet washed. So each person washes and is washed, demonstrating reciprocity and exchange, humility and blessing. Though I've attended several of these Thursday services, I have yet to go be part of the foot-washing ritual. Unsure about what holds me back, I trust that if I am to do this, I will know at the time. Then I will do as all those who participate do—leave my shoes in the pew, take off my socks, and join the file of barefooted worshippers already sure they want to perform this act. My role thus far has been to witness this event in the old sense of that word, i.e., to testify to its validity and authenticity. I am present in the moment, watching attentively as each person washes or has his or her feet washed, and, in so doing, I lend credence to the ritualized action. Also, I am called to have compassion towards those participating as they repeat and thereby enliven a practice going back to the historical Jesus.

On Good Friday, I usually attend two services: the Celebration of the Lord's Passion in the afternoon, and the *Tenebrae* service in the late evening. The Basilica stages a multi-parted Passion service, including the Liturgy of the Word presented as a vocal rendering of the Passion according to St. John; showing and communal veneration of the Cross; extended intercessions; Holy Communion; and a concluding prayer. After this liturgy is concluded, there is an opportunity for individual veneration of the cross.

Going to the Passion service meets several of my criteria for how to practice my beliefs. The ritual never changes its format; it brings me into close connection with what Jesus experienced over 2,000 years ago; it speaks to several of my senses (sight, hearing, touch, feeling); and it places me squarely within a community of people who believe in a God who took flesh, lived among other human beings, was tried and crucified in order to demonstrate magnanimous love. After a rendering of the Gospel according to John, which includes the interrogation, trial, and crucifixion of Jesus, we listen to general intercessions read out by a member of the congregation and responded to by us with "Lord, hear our prayer." Then several strong adult males unhook the large wooden cross from its position in the exact center of the church where it has hung throughout Lent, reminding us as we enter of the drama that will unfold at the end of our forty-day period of preparation. This cross, made of planks two inches wide and six inches long, stained dark brown with equally dark red edges, measures an impressive seven feet by four feet.

The choir has positioned itself on either side of the outside aisles, so their singing surrounds us. The cross-carriers take the massive, red-tinted rood to each of the four directional archways of the building, and we repeat an invitation and response about the meaning of death on the cross. The celebrant chants "This is the wood of the cross, on which hung the Savior of the world" and we reply "Come let us worship." The cross is then raised by the carriers who hand it over the heads of one quadrant of the congregation. Each person lifts his or her hands to try and touch the cross as it makes its diagonal way to the center aisle where it is held aloft and carried to the next archway. This forceful ritual is repeated in the east, west, north, and south sections of our cathedral so that most of the people attending have an opportunity to touch the cross. I have figured out just where to sit in order to insure being able to reach up and help the cross travel above me. In this way, I symbolically and momentarily relieve Jesus from having to bear alone the entire burden of Calvary. As my hands feel for a second the cold, hard surface of that giant object, I experience deep pain for what others just like me and the people gathered around me did to such a good man long ago. Once the cross has traveled above our heads, its carriers take it right up to the high altar at the front of the basilica sanctuary where they install it in an upright position for the remainder of the service. At the very end, they take it down and rest it on the steps leading up to the sanctuary as the celebrant invites any who wish to do so to come forward to perform an individual veneration.

My first two times at this service, I held back, telling myself it was not "sanitary" to kiss the surface that is then only casually wiped by a small cloth. The third time, I surrendered to the moment and went up. I'd noticed that year a man near the beginning of the procession who just touched the cross with his hand, so I was emboldened to go forward but not to put my lips on the wood. As I got closer, my heart sped up, and my hands broke into a sweat. Clearly, I was supposed to be doing this symbolic act. From some essential part of me, I knew exactly what to do when it was my "turn." I knelt and rested my forehead against the cross and said a quiet "amen." Because there were many others behind me, I got up much sooner than I would have preferred. I wanted to stay kneeling at the contemporary marker for the instrument of torture and death endured by Jesus. As I silently spoke a few words from this position as a supplicant, I knew what I really wanted to do was prostrate myself at the base of the cross and sob out my grief. I wanted to say "Oh, Jesus, help me remember more often and more acutely the pain you endured in order to give me a new and loving way to feel about God."

Most people quietly left the church once they had completed their act of veneration, but I slipped into a pew near the back and knelt until the very last person had participated. Instead of prostrating myself on the cold floor, I sang the repetitive verse we had been enjoined to chant at the beginning of the veneration process, half an hour earlier: "Stay with me,/Remain here with me,/Watch and pray,/Watch and pray." Sung in a minor key, the repetition seems to become more powerful as it sinks further into my consciousness, and then it haunts me all through the next twenty-four hours, as if it had aural or spiritual energy lingering around it, a kind of invisible inertia. My staying until the last member of the congregation had walked up to the cross meant that I was subjugating my own preference to sit comfortably in my pew or, better yet, to go home and have my light supper, to something bigger than myself. In a way, that subjugation of self lies at the very heart of Jesus' time on the way to and at Calvary. After all, he had asked God, who was also his mystical father, to let the cup pass him by if possible; he didn't embrace death immediately or unquestioningly, since he had much good work that he could have continued to do had he lived longer. But finally he accepted his ending as the only story in which he was to take part. That's who he "is" to me—someone who could live and work amidst uncertainties, doubts, and pain without reaching for easy resolution or answers. The 19th century English poet, John Keats, called this special ability "negative capability." Jesus' acceptance of his death also

embodies the ideas behind the Serenity Prayer said at every Twelve
Step meeting, in which we ask for the ability to accept the things
we cannot change, the courage to change the things we can, and
(crucially) the wisdom to know the difference. So Jesus' last days
demonstrate for me his utter humanity because he hoped he might
not have to die, and his utter divinity because he surrendered to the
cross as his final "place" in the hearts of his followers.

Good Friday includes a second service in the evening called
Tenebrae or Shadows. This is a solemn observance of a world without
the light of Jesus in it. Traditionally, it has also been an anti-Semitic
moment in the liturgy, since the biblical readings accent that it
was Jews who called for Christ's death on the cross. In order to
resist perpetuating such slanderous and divisive comments, some
churches have rewritten that part of the service, making it clear
that Jesus himself was an observant and faithful Jew. My church
adds a personal element by inviting a rabbi from one of the urban
synagogues to worship with us and deliver the talk from the pulpit.
In this homily, we are reminded of what unites us—Christians, Jews,
and Muslims—we all recognize Abraham as the bedrock figure in
our religious histories. For me, given my predilection for dramatic
rituals, the important part of this service comes near the end. After
each appointed reading from Scripture, an acolyte snuffs out one
candle burning in the sanctuary, decreasing thereby the amount of
light by a fraction. As this symbolic act is performed, a technician at
the back of the basilica very slowly dims the lighting system for the
whole massive space in which we are gathered.

At the very end of the service, we find ourselves in a barely lit
church, only one burning candle remaining. Someone goes up to the
chancel, takes that candle in his or her hands, and slowly walks down
the long nave, taking away the last vestige of light even as the lighting
system moves to zero. The candle-bearer takes that thin sliver of light
into the narthex. We are left in utter darkness. After a few minutes
of experiencing that absence, we begin to beat our hands on the tops
of our wooden pews. Given the superb acoustics at the Basilica, this
action on the part of several hundred people makes a huge racket,
calling to mind the earthquake that is said to have occurred after
Jesus had been crucified. Our noisy gesture signals that we as a
congregation are insisting that the light return so that we do not

remain hopeless in the face of colossal loss. After several minutes of pounding, the lone person reenters the church and slowly walks up the long center aisle with the single candle. Once into the sanctuary, s/he replaces the tiny candle on the altar and leaves. We all exit the basilica in solemn silence, heartened by even the slightest glow from that lone and lonely candle. The shadows or *tenebrae* surround us, and we prepare for the Easter Vigil on Saturday evening.

When we are in the dark, I usually recall a wonderful essay by Virginia Woolf in which she writes about what it was like for her to witness a total eclipse of the sun: "The shadow growing darker and darker over the moor was like the heeling over of a boat, which, instead of righting itself at the critical moment, turns a little further and then a little further on its side; and suddenly capsizes. So the light turned and heeled over and went out. This was the end. The flesh and blood of the world was dead; only the skeleton was left.... Lightly on the other side of the world, up it rose.... Never was there such a sense of rejuvenescence and recovery" (from the essay, "The Sun and the Fish"). My placement of Woolf within the Good Friday service surely is a lovely reprise of my needing to "believe" in her when first I was trying to stay sober and attend Alcoholics Anonymous. The darkness of *tenebrae*, like Virginia's experience of the eclipse, can be healing if I concentrate on what mystics like St. John of the Cross have taught me about the necessary descent into darkness if I want any real apprehension of the great light of understanding and divine inspiration. And while I beat my palms as vigorously as my neighbors, I also am in touch with an inner calm that assures me that I can find new meaning if I step out of the various light sources offered to me by the secular world. So many people today are like rabbits caught in the headlights of an on-coming car—they are mesmerized by the sheer power of the glow, and so follow it to their own peril and often destruction. I think of the people who want to be on so-called reality shows, or people who fabricate situations to get a few minutes of media attention, or those who seem to relish appearing on confessional television programs where they tell millions of invisible and total strangers some of the most intimate and painful aspects of their lives. Spending time in that kind of spotlight prevents a person from truly seeing themselves or their world. I much prefer soft lights and candles, avoiding neon whenever possible. Dusk and dawn are powerful times in a day for me because boundaries are fuzzied then, becoming liminal or "thin spaces," as they are sometimes described. As the sharper lines seen in the morning or afternoon dim, the veil between earth and spirit becomes just a tiny bit more transparent, even if only fleetingly.

At the Vigil on the Saturday before Easter itself, the Basilica stages a marathon service, lasting about three and a half hours, beginning at 8 p.m. At this service, the new Light of Christ or Easter candle is brought into a dark church from outside where it has been lighted from a distinctly pagan bonfire set burning in a large cauldron placed at the base of the Basilica plaza. Several scriptural readings take place, beginning with the heptameral Creation story in Genesis. We also listen to Abraham's test by God to see if he is willing to kill his own son to obey God, and to Moses' parting of the Red Sea because his God wants the Israealites to flee the Egyptians. Finally we hear the prophetic voice of Isaiah, promising the coming of a Messiah, predicting the rejection of that figure by the secular powers who are threatened by his message of love and forgiveness, generosity and justice. As the readers recount these founding stories, musical accompaniment helps create an aura, sometimes of peacefulness as at the time of creation, other times of the wrath of God in the Red Sea scene. Every year, during the Genesis account of the creation, I find myself going along happily as God makes the universe and its myriad creatures. Then we come to words the writer of this initial book of the Hebrew scriptures has God say to humans: the words "dominion" and "rule" enter what has been a space of plenitude and harmony. I want to stand up and shout, "NO, this is a huge mistake." I believe telling humans we have dominion over all creation has played a central part in wars and bigotry and, now, to the possible extinction of all the beautiful things created and found 'good' in this powerful story of beginnings.

Eventually, young people are confirmed into the church, those wishing to become Roman Catholic are baptized through immersion, and adults coming to the Catholic church from other denominations are welcomed into their new spiritual home. At the end of these initiation rites, mass is celebrated. When all these rituals are over, I feel both uplifted and exhausted. I have been part of an arc that has traveled from triumphant and laudatory welcome, through agony into a horrible death, and finally, a promise of lasting victory. If I tried to experience this trajectory alone, it wouldn't work because it is the very act of communal observance that adds power to the words and gestures. My church is filled for all the Triduum services, as it is for Palm Sunday, and it is in these numbers that I find a strange sense of place. Waving my palm frond, listening to the Passion of St. John, touching the cross's wood as other congregants' hands do the same, kneeling at that same cross, witnessing the entry into the church of new communicants, and finally belting out, "Jesus Christ is risen today, halleluia!"—this is what I missed most during all the years I stayed away from any organized religious services. And being part of this communal practice is what sustains and uplifts me as I go forward on my very personal faith journey, ironic as that may seem.

If I compare my full participation in these Triduum services, where part of the power of the moment comes from being part of a large community, with my experience of a "community" of just two as I sat under the adolescent chimpanzee as he finished his breakfast, I begin to understand that I can find my God in a variety of settings that may seem contradictory at first glance but which are simply paradoxical, hence incapable of easy resolution.

Chapter 9
Commonplace Books

*I*n the 14th century, Italians began publishing a new kind of book called a *zibaldone* or "hodgepodge" book. These books were informal, smaller than the more official volumes being published at the time, and containing a wide variety of poetry and prose. Family recipes were found next to quotations from the Bible; tax records jostled lines from Virgil; currency exchange rates were listed next to names of grandchildren. By the 1600s, this practice of collecting all sorts of mixed trivia had given way in England to collections of quotations and personal axioms recorded for private consumption. Such activity was called "commonplacing" and the collections came to be knows as "commonplace books." Writers were especially fond users of such olios, sometimes even admitting that they drew on items from their commonplace book when they sat down to do their more formal and literary composing. Today, most literary and cultural critics see such artifacts as extremely valuable for the light they shed on the tastes or trains of thought held by a given author that can be deduced from entries in a commonplace book.

As I continue, in my seventies, to wrestle with the contours of my relationship to God and God's relationship to the universe, I find myself making mini-commonplace books. Because books of all sorts have always provided me with a way to understand my realities, I currently rely on some of them for spiritual fodder. During the writing of this memoir, I've collected brief quotations from written and spoken sources that have at the time of reading or hearing seemed germane to my project. I want now to place some of those commonplace entries into this text and see what happens.

During a recent Lenten season, I chose for my theological reading one of Rabbi Abraham Heschel's works, *God in Search of Man*. To my delight, much of his argument is framed around his understanding of two distinct strains of thought in western culture— the classical and the biblical. By the classical he means, of course, our inheritance from the Greeks. Heschel documents how these thinkers asserted that humans could know the universe if we but studied and experimented and experienced deeply enough. Contrarily, the biblical inheritance turns on a fundamental assertion that humans never can know everything and, indeed, may truly know very little. As I kept reading this engrossing work, it became clear to me that by "biblical" the rabbi was not thinking of the Gospel writers or the author of Revelations. His "biblical" meant the Hebrew bible, filled with writings by major (and a few minor) prophets, each of whom was seeking God.

This excellent source work is replete with quotations from that Hebrew Bible, all of which confirm Heschel's thesis that we will always wind up standing before that which is hidden, ineffable, and unknowable. As a confirmed feminist, the biblical mind is much more familiar to and congruent with my own thinking, so at every turn in my reading, I find myself nodding or saying out loud "yes" to the Hebraic side of Heschel's comparative assertions.

A friend of mine, who has spent many years working with police and other agencies involved in criminal justice while practicing her deep religious beliefs as an ordained minister, has printed an unusual day-by-day book. She has a month's worth of short reflections that include a Bible verse relevant to a story gleaned from her contacts with people living *in extremis*. In one of my favorites, she has this sentence: "Perhaps it is in the horizontal arm of the cross that the vertical is incarnated." Coming upon this, I was unable to keep reading for a time. A few months before, I had a conversation with another friend interested in early depictions of the Crucifixion scene. We were discussing the fact that in early English Christian churches, the cross above the altar was a simple rood. Jesus did not begin to appear as the crucified Christ figure until after the 9th century. For my own part, I am always drawn to empty crosses in my travels, so I posited to my friend that the lateral part of crosses perhaps signified humans' relationship to the divine—a vertical matter—while the longitudinal arm stood for humans' relationships with one another—a horizontal matter. I further suggested that Jesus represented the intersection or combination of both since he was simultaneously God and human, so placing him at the intersection of the two arms of any cross affirmed his dual nature. My friend's work with street people, who are powerful representatives of the horizontal world, had touched something in her to connect her with the vertical world of faith.

Another tiny entry in my recent spiritual commonplace book comes from a hymn written by John B. Geyer. Singing this hymn as the Basilica choir recessed down the long nave at church, I was stopped by this line: "The Spirit's fission shakes the Church of God." My immediate understanding of "fission" comes from atomic physics. Fission describes that process in which the nucleus of an atom splits into smaller parts, often producing free neutrons and photons. This is an exothermic reaction releasing large amounts of kinetic energy, so the person who wrote the appealing line in the hymn wants to convey just how powerful the Holy Spirit can be. Since the physics phenomenon always results in the release of new energies, I imagine those of us who respond to the Holy Spirit as converting our initial awe into smaller but life-changing actions. Also, given the strength of nuclear fission, the verb "shakes" suggests to me a force of earthquake proportions. Since the Church of God can become both mammoth and moribund over time, it often requires a force of great magnitude to change it. Vatican II was such a moment in the Roman Catholic Church, as was the moment when the Episcopal bishops finally voted to ordain women priests, or when Martin Luther posted his theses on the church door in Wittenberg, Germany in 1517.

What does spiritual fission mean in my own personal life? I have felt a breaking up of my staunch resistance to the Holy Spirit over the past few years, a breaking open of my heart as it has been healing from being traumatized by the loss of my life partner of twenty-seven years. I am shaken by the Spirit's fission, and it may have needed something that powerful to soften my defenses against my own special "noisome pestilences." And, while I have not joined large movements to help those in need, I have changed how I relate to other people I meet along my day-to-day path. Most importantly, I am open to my better impulses and my softer feelings, and I experience surges of energy in response to beauty as well as tragedy in the world around me.

This newly freed energy must be why I entered in my spiritual commonplace book this line from one of the hypnotic Taizé verses: "summon out what I shall be." When we sang that in church one Sunday, as we walked up the aisle to take communion, I found myself in tears, a usual sign of a breaking down of my resistance and an opening up to the spirit of God. This phrase is all about a longing to become more of what we might be, about getting out of our own light, or praying to have our shortcomings removed so that we can shine without becoming blinded by ego. The use of the formal "shall" assures us that, as we sing it over and over, we will be able to hear and heed the summons when it comes. If I ask myself when do I currently feel closest to the person I "shall be" some day, the answer comes easily: in my garden, engrossed in the beautiful language of flowers that enlarges my empathic abilities; in church on my knees or singing loudly if not always tonally; in the presence of large and sublime nature; writing on those days when the words seem to want to spring from my mind or heart.

What these situations just described have in common is striking: all of them find me in that state of being I now understand as solitude. Different from aloneness, solitude is for me creative space, space where I am momentarily freed from various kinds of distractions, even those that are positive. I think of all the Shakespeare plays in which characters need to go to a forest, or a wood, or an island, or some other semi-magical space in order to find or regain their centers. They then are returned to their social spaces, most often families or courts, capable of behaving better than they had been doing before their hegiras. Or I think of the desert fathers, men who lived entirely apart from others human beings, in order to be channels for prophetic knowledge.

Our current culture seems to fear solitude over almost all else except terrorist attacks. Cell phones, iPods, Blackberries, Face Book, play stations, iPads—all these and myriad other technological devices and spaces keep many of us constantly "hooked" to other people or events or images or sounds. Once it was the case that everyone was forced to sink into themselves in certain situations like airplane flights or walking around a lake or riding a bus or doing the grocery shopping alone or sitting in a doctor's office. Now, with a touch of a screen or the flick of a button we can be "saved" from whatever thoughts or feelings might arise from such silences.

Many years ago when I first began to battle the demon inside me that believed food could mask all my unpleasant feelings and blunt all my pain, someone suggested that I make a little sign and tape it to the door of my refrigerator. It read, "Your mother is not inside." Aside from my computer and Google, I own and participate in none of the current so-called aids to social networking precisely because I am quite sure that the God of my understanding is not "inside" Face Book or YouTube. Surely I can see God in human friends, neighbors, and even strangers, but it is in solitude that I most often establish close and deep connection with the presence I recognize as my Higher Power.

Books populate that solitude with language that, in turn, sends me further inside to contact places in me that lie dormant much of the time but that can be enlivened by what someone else has said. That is why the concept of commonplace books so appeals to me. Recently, I came across a quotation by Alice Walker that I had typed onto a 4x6 index card years ago. I know it was long ago because the card is yellowed and curled at its four corners. The quotation appears in Walker's novel, *The Temple of My Familiar*, a story in which a girl named Lissie develops a powerful relationship with her "familiar," who is part bird, part fish, and part reptile, small enough to fit into Lissie's hand, full of mischief while also being capable of providing protection. This is also the story of Africans fighting against overwhelmingly vicious oppressors. What made the strongest impression on me when I first read the novel, some time in the early 1990s, is this: "If you tear out the tongue of another, you have a tongue in your hand the rest of your life. You are responsible, therefore, for all that person might have said" (*The Temple of My Familiar*, Harcourt Brace Jovanovich, San Diego, 1989, p. 310-11). Spoken in the context of Walker's description of a merciless political revolt, these words found their way into my consciousness.

Reading them now, I believe they define part of my own ethic, since they warn me against silencing other voices. All the years I taught students at the University of Minnesota, I tried to listen to what they found moving or troubling about the books we studied rather than simply imposing my own interpretations. My initial reason for assuming this pedagogical posture stemmed from my own experience in classes from grammar school through college and even a master's program. My raised hand most often was ignored entirely, proving once again that benign neglect can be debilitating. When I was called upon, often my reading of a play or novel or poem was shown to be tangential, overly emotional, or just plain "wrong." Because I learned to silence myself in order to avoid yet another embarrassing and painful put-down, when I was in a position of academic authority, I vowed not to reproduce that paradigm with my students.

The one time when I was unable to remain faithful to this hard-won tenet occurred when I taught Shakespeare's sonnets while still a closeted lesbian. A male graduate student asked me, in class, whether I thought there might be an implicit intimate relationship between the poet and the young man to whom eighty percent of the poems were written. Terrified by this probably innocent query, I launched into a rapid-fire explanation of Platonic friendship as it was revived during the Renaissance, stressing that such friendships were superior to heterosexual liaisons because there was no sexual element. I knew I was lying, since I was convinced that those 127 amazing sonnets described a complex web of emotions and behaviors arising from deep intimacy on a sexual as well as companionate level.

Decades after this shameful moment that caused me immediate and repeated regret, a sentence came to me that I have kept, thinking to write a poem one day in which it would be the opening line: "If I'm in the closet, you're in the dark." Surely my inability to respond honestly to that inquisitive young man kept him and the rest of the students uninformed about what actually was being explored by The

Bard. The better ending to this shabby story turns around the fact that I was still teaching Shakespeare after I came out at the University, so later students were enlightened because I was able to step out of my putatively protective closet and tell them the truth as I saw it.

Many recent entries in my spiritual commonplace book come from the Psalms, biblical texts that have always appealed to me and that are becoming part of the Bible to which I return regularly. A good friend, with whom I share my writing and she hers, is about to embark on a rereading of the psalms because she finds such beauty and solace in them. I've spoken here about asking my mother and father, when just a child, to tell me their favorite psalm, and I've acknowledged that my absolute favorite is Psalm 91. Because there is a choral presentation of an appointed psalm every Sunday at the Basilica, I hear many more than has been true in the past. Psalm 42, stands out these days, and begins: "Like as the hart desireth the water-brooks, so longest my soul after thee, O God. My soul is athirst for God, the living God: when shall I come to appear before the presence of God?" (This is the wording in my trusted copy of Thomas Cranmer's *Book of Common Prayer*). This stirring opener is worded slightly differently by Rabbi Abraham Heschel in his profoundly evocative book *God in Search of Man*:

> As a hart yearns for the streams of water,
> So does my soul yearn for Thee, O God.
> My soul thirsts for God, the living God,
> When shall I come and see the face of the Lord?

Finally, Don Krubsak, composer-in-residence at the Basilica and life-partner of the choir director there, has written a piece sung during Lent, especially at the Easter Vigil. The refrain returns to Psalm 42: "Like a deer that longs for running water, my soul longs for thee."

I once wrote a brief and overly "talky" essay on my understanding of what constituted yearning. The essay was a dud, but my continuing fascination with the concept helps explain why this psalmic verse affects me so strongly. To yearn or to long for is to admit a sharp absence of that quality or person or place. It also denotes something beyond mere wanting or even needing. The process that David, the psalmist, is writing about involves a human being's deepest desire for spiritual union with the divine. Yet he uses a markedly commonplace metaphor through which to express this feeling. In usual circumstances, deer in the forest make their way to the nearest brook, stream, or river each morning and evening in order to keep themselves hydrated and healthy. David's deer surely has not had such an easy supply source, hence the "longing" or "yearning" for that precious water. The metaphor works because the deer in question is in physical extremis, just as the human being without God may find herself in spiritual extremis.

I have felt the absence of sustaining soul nourishment at many moments over my lifetime, so when I hear and sing these words, my heart responds fully and deeply. If I ask myself where my watery oases are today, the answer is not always clear. Sometimes, I find the longed-for "water" in church, practicing the sacramental liturgies that connect me to a loving power outside myself. Often, however, it is in external nature that I seek and find soul comfort. Earlier in this memoir, I describe my profound sense that "God" is in the water cascading with such mighty force at Niagara Falls or, more recently, is embedded in the forests and plains of Tanzania. These "places" are sublime and spectacular, locations I can return to in memory to reclaim the cleansing and refreshing process experienced when literally in their midst. But such moments cannot sustain me over the long haul since, like the deer in the psalm, I long for that "running water" all the time. The spiritual implication surely involves my discovering more places where the God of my understanding can be found if I'm willing to look a little deeper or harder.

In Minneapolis, we are blessed with a wild flower garden originally designed and maintained by two local teachers who shared a life with one another for many years. This place, the Eloise Butler Wild Flower Garden, is tucked away at the edge of the city near one of our many lake havens. I walk its familiar paths almost every spring, finding healing presence among the trout lilies, May apples, swamp cabbage, bloodroot, and a variety of worts. This local place contains "running water" that never fails to refresh me, no matter how many times I go there to commune with the flowers and shrubs and to listen to the birds who escape urban noise and pressures in the old, knarled trees growing in this secluded space. What I have learned over my years of visiting this garden is that some of the most beautiful flowers can be overlooked, literally, because they are so tiny and close to the ground that the casual stroller doesn't notice them. I often find myself on my knees, not accidentally, peeking under or around some leaves or other camouflage to discover tiny hepatica blooms or the red under-flowers of the ginger root. In those moments, I understand that I am longing to see into the secret heart of external natural beauty and, in that search, I mirror my yearning for more revelations of God's beneficence.

The psalms often speak to my need to affirm that my higher power is aware of my existence and can be called upon for help in times of trouble. One such instance occurs in Psalm 102, parts of which figure in how we in the congregation respond to a moment in the liturgy of *Tenebrae*, observed on the night of Good Friday: "I have become like a pelican in the wilderness, my bones burn away like fire, I lie awake and I moan like some lonely bird on a roof." I was so moved by this phrase the first time I heard it that I went home and immediately read the whole psalm, discovering that the liturgist had made a pastiche from several verses of the original.

The scholar in me is convinced that we get the most when we go to the earliest source and sink into its language. Here is the section of Psalm 102 from which the single response has been shaped: "Hear my prayer, O Lord, and let my cry come until thee./Hide not thy face from me to the day when I am in trouble; incline thine ear unto me; in the day when I call answer me speedily./For my days are consumed like smoke, and my bones are burned as an hearth./ My heart is smitten, and withered like grass; so that I forget to eat my bread./By reason of the voice of my groaning my bones cleave to my skin./I am like a pelican of the wilderness; I am like an owl of the desert./I watch, and am as a sparrow alone upon the house top." Surely the speaker of these lines pleads for the Lord to hear him in his greatest need, not to leave him stranded and distracted to the point of forgetting even to eat. The places named here encompass huge geographical and human living situations—wilderness and desert suggest extreme geographies where a person desperately needs to feel God's nearness. But a house top is among the commonest of locales, so the speaker needs God as much when he is amidst company as when he feels cut off from humanity.

Like the psalmist, I want a faith that serves me in all my various locations. For years, I only called on the God I was taught to imagine when my life was going badly, and I needed some sense that it would change for the better. So I bargained, promising this God all sorts of tangible services such as going to church more often or increasing my contribution level when next asked to pledge. If I got what I prayed for, often as not I forgot what I'd offered as my part of the deal; and, even if I remembered it, my fidelity to doing it waned amazingly fast. As I read more contemplative literature and consider just what force is the focus of my current belief, I realize that I'm no longer praying for specific outcomes for me or even for those close to me.

Rather today, when I kneel or sit quietly or think while walking every morning, I put myself and those I love into an imagined atmosphere full of light and often harmonic sounds. The phrases that go through my mind most often at such times are amorphous but heartfelt: "Let Jane find peace as she keeps trying to make a new life without her beloved partner"; "Keep the Obamas safe this day and let him not lose his way"; "Help me remain open to what this day brings without grasping or regretting or sinking into self-pity."

These and like phrases are addressed no longer to a "being," male or female. They go out into a universe that has infinite care for me and everyone else, into a spiritual space made up of love and compassion for all living organisms, even those I cannot bring myself to appreciate when I actually see them in my garden or on a nature program on educational television.

Some of my most recent additions to my spiritual commonplace book are again from one of Rabbi Abraham Heschel's books, *God in Search of Man*. For years, I have known his name as a leading Jewish theologian and author but had never actually read his work. Recently, I was listening to the last portion of NPR's "Speaking of Faith," with Krista Tippett. She was speaking with a young rabbinical scholar who was there to celebrate Rabbi Heschel's contributions to twentieth-century thought. He said of all the rabbi's works, he was partial to *God in Search of Man*, and I thought to myself, "He's misspoken because he's nervous about being on national radio—surely the title is *Man in Search of God*."

When, the next day, I went on line to my university library, I discovered that the young man may well have been nervous, but he was correct about the title. Intrigued, I ordered up the book which I read avidly upon its arrival at my home. Heschel explains the title by declaring that God is indeed always looking for us, pointing out the following: "When Adam and Eve hid from His presence, the Lord called: *Where art thou* (Genesis 3:9).... Religion consists of God's question and man's answer. The way *to* faith is the way *of* faith. The way to God is the way of God. Unless God asks the question, all our inquiries are in vain" (p.137).

Each time Heschel posed his two world views—the scientific that searches for answers to life's mysteries, and the prophetic that stands in awe of life's mysteries—I found myself squarely on the side of the prophets. Quotations I added to my collection all reflect this fundamental difference in approach. For instance, early in the work, Heschel writes: "Nature as a tool box is a world that does not point beyond itself. It is when nature is sensed as mystery and grandeur that it calls upon us to look beyond it.... We teach children how to measure, how to weigh. We fail to teach them how to revere, how to sense wonder and awe" (p.36). A few pages further along, I found this passage that seemed to put into words exactly how I feel: "The sublime is that which we see and are unable to convey. It is the silent allusion of things to a meaning greater than themselves.... It is that which our words, our forms, our categories can never reach. This is why the sense of the sublime must be regarded as the root of man's [sic] creative activities in art, thought, and noble living" (p. 39). Clearly this man of faith believes that science is extremely valuable in delineating our universe and framing its complexities. It is just as clear that he finds his own strength and reality from stepping aside from such calculations in order to affirm awe and surprise in the face of the ineffable.

In two passages, Heschel makes his distinction entirely plain: "Modern man dwells upon the order and power of nature; the prophets dwell upon the grandeur and creation of nature. The former directs his attention to the manageable and intelligible aspect of the universe; the latter to its mystery and marvel" (p.97); and "There seem to be two courses of human thinking: one begins with man and his needs and ends in assuming that the universe is a meaningless display and a waste of energy; the other begins in amazement, in awe and humility and ends in the assumption that the universe is full of a glory that surpasses man and his mind, but is of eternal meaning to Him who made being possible" (p.105).

What the rabbinical scholar is trying to get me to understand is that some things resist our systems of explanation and analysis; they are ineffable, hence shrouded in mystery. Our proper posture in such situations is wonder, not skepticism or even frantic searchings for answers. I need no longer write pages to my mother, or anyone else, about Jesus' meaning in the world, as I did when much younger. Heschel's writings also affirm my conviction that faith lies outside doctrinal systems or creeds, preferring to harbor in our hearts rather than to appeal to our sense of conformity or our trust in knowledge.

His treatise has also proven helpful as I continue to understand how my own faith system is working. Heschel claims at one point in his argument that faith is not easy to attain: "A decision of the will, the desire to believe, will not secure it. All the days of our lives we must continue to deepen our sense of mystery in order to be worthy of attaining faith. Callousness to the mystery is our greatest obstacle. In the artificial light of pride and self-contentment we shall never see the splendor. Only *in His light shall we see light*" (p.153). The italicized portion speaks to the very essence of mysticism, even as it holds out the possibility of humans' merging with the divine. Henry Vaughan, the 17th century metaphysical poet, began one of his most famous poems with these words: "I saw eternity the other night/ Like a ring of pure and endless light." He would agree with the rabbi about the ultimate source of splendor.

My penultimate moment of connection with Heschel came near the end of his extraordinary book as he talked about all the references of God's appearing in or from a cloud, first of all to Moses to whom he said: "Lo, I am coming to you *in the thickness of a cloud*." Heschel believes this motif "unequivocally conveys to the mind the fundamental truth that God was *concealed* even when He *revealed*, that even while his voice became manifest His essence remained hidden" (p. 193). What I like about this concept is its paradoxical nature. My faith system is based on the tantamount paradox within Christianity itself, i.e., Christ is fully human and Christ is fully divine. At various moments in temporal history, theologians have worried this idea, some seeing Christ as monolithic, hence either only human or only divine. For me, such debates stem from thinking the two-sidedness is a contradiction rather than a paradox. Contradictions can be "decided," one way or the other—it either is raining or it is not raining, it cannot be both raining and not raining. Paradoxes, on the other hand, cannot be resolved one way or the other. We must simply try to accept them and live within the uncomfortable mystery they create. Since ambiguity has never appealed to the majority of North Americans, paradoxes are avoided or contorted into something simpler that can be settled and then dismissed.

Late in his argument about God's being in search of us humans, Heschel shares his own sense of prophetic time and how it differs from secular notions of time. For his objective correlative, he chooses what happened on Mount Sinai, asserting that that moment is both an event that actually occurred at a specific time in history and an event that repeats itself all the time. "What God does, happens both in time and in eternity. Seen from our vantage point, it happened once; seen from His vantage point, it happens all the time. Monuments of stone are destined to disappear; days of spirit never pass away." He takes as his Biblical evidence of this gigantic paradox a passage in Genesis 19:1 in which the writer says the Torah was presented the third month AFTER other events, but then asserts that it was given "on *this* day." As Heschel points out, grammatical and spatial logic dictates that the sentence should have read: "on *that* day." However, Heschel has been at pains throughout his book to distinguish between a scientific and a prophetic approach to the universe and its history. So he sees the author of Genesis as merely affirming a prophetic truth, i.e., the day of giving the Torah can never become past. When I read this sentence, I flashed to William Faulkner's words spoken when accepting the Nobel Prize for literature in 1950. He asserts at one point, "The past is never passed." Faulkner would understand Heschel's theory of time's not being linear for people struggling with how to live in this world. So for Heschel "that" day when the Torah was presented to Moses is "this" day and every other day. The Torah, whenever someone studies it, must be "as if it were given us today." Prophetic time, then, is not linear or finite; rather it is eternal and spontaneous and ever-present.

When I taught literature at the University of Minnesota, I tried to help students see the magic of the gerundive case in relation to time. Gerunds, verb forms ending in "ing," put action into an eternal present tense. To say "I am walking" suggests something continuing into the moment of speaking, whereas to say "I walk" or "I walked" or "I will walk" or "I have walked" all limit time to some particular moment in an assumed present, past, or future. I wanted them to see that a poet who casts action in the gerundive case wants us readers to enter into that action, making whatever the poet is describing a part of our own present as well as something that occurred once at a specific moment. This poetic device shares Rabbi Heschel's goal of lifting history out of a static or frozen zone and breathing immediacy and intimacy into events that might otherwise seem distant or "dated." A friend tells me that in Greek, there is an aorist tense that conveys the sense that past action is ongoing rather than being over with or safely in the past.

That's what God is for me these days—a force or energy field no longer "placed" anywhere but rather miraculously accessible to me most often through mundane and small details in my life and world. My God, then, is immanent rather than transcendent, available to me through the most commonplace details as readily as within the realm of the ineffable. And that God demands that I participate ever more fully in the life around me, never escaping into some platonic realm of abstraction.

Chapter 10
Excitement and the Spirit

*A*s I continue in my seventies to ponder the contours of my faith, new stimuli surface and call me into deeper contemplation. Surprisingly, one of these stimuli has recently revolved around my long-time interest in puffins.

In early July of 2010, I flew to Reykjavik, Iceland, where I spent my first two days as a *flaneuse*, walking in the inner city, observing what was around me, stumbling upon geographical "gifts," letting myself absorb the texture and feel of the strangely named streets and stores. On the third morning, I connected with a tour guide who had agreed to drive just me up the west coast to the northernmost part of the country where many fjords exist. It wasn't the fingers of water that I was seeking, however; it was a cliff named Landsjbarj that many thousands of puffins call home during mating, nesting, and fledgling season.

As the time approached to go, friends asked me if I were excited, and I replied immediately and enthusiastically "yes." Upon reflection, I realized that I had not used that word for any activity in which I was about to engage since my life partner initiated our break-up.

Those compact little sea birds with the bright beaks so often pictured full of tiny, limp fish opened me back up to excitement. I often point out that for Shakespeare, being able to experience and feel wonder as an adult is one sure measure of goodness in a character. Often in describing myself over the years since I sobered up, I have owned my own capacity for wonder as one of my most shining attributes.

My fascination with puffins began many years ago when my partner and I took a summer holiday in Southwest Harbor, Maine. Taking advice from a friend, we rented a room at a turn-of-the-20th century hotel named The Claremont. The old classic green and white frame building had a large common room with a huge fireplace, a dining room with three sides in windows looking down the greensward to the oceanfront, and rooms upstairs. A brochure offered by the hotel boasted a newly formed colony of Atlantic puffins visible in summer in their native island habitat off the Maine coast. The colored image on the front of the brochure caught my attention: two little birds with carnival bright beaks were pictured. Upon reading the brochure, I found myself wanting to try to go to the island. For several summers after that, my partner and I toyed with making the crossing by rowboat from a coastal town about an hour from our hotel. We never made that trip because of the inconvenience of needing to arise about 3:00 a.m. in order to drive to the little town to get the boat, and because the boat service told us over the telephone that if the water was too choppy in the late afternoon, they would not fetch us back to the mainland. The prospect, even dim, of having to spend a night in a bird blind with no bedding or facilities held us back.

In the process, however, of debating the adventure of going to Matinicus Island, I discovered that it was possible to become a member of Project Puffin, an organization of the Maine Audubon Society dedicated to raising funds to support those who were intent upon enlarging the virtually extinct colony that had once spent summers on that jutting rock unpopulated by humans. I adopted a puffin, EN 53, and have been her "mother" ever since. In 2010, she turned 32, and she and her mate have successfully fledged their single, carefully nurtured egg all but two of the last twenty years. My bond with her is sufficiently strong to prompt me to think of her fairly often, especially during summers when I know she and her mate are working hard to secure little fishes for their growing puffling—the real name for a baby puffin.

While EN53 became a vibrant photograph that I studied often, I continued to long to see breathing puffins. So, one night when I changed over from watching a DVD to television and caught the end of a program about a photographer in my home state of Minnesota who had gone around the entire coast of Iceland taking photographs, I was mesmerized by several images of puffins sitting calmly or flying vigorously around cliff faces at the ocean side. Next morning, I Googled "Iceland puffins" and was rewarded with several sites boasting more puffins on that one island than anywhere in the whole world. Following my long-time dream, I then searched the Internet for "Iceland puffins small tours." This request yielded four entries from men who worked as guides taking groups of fewer than ten people to various Icelandic locations. I was most taken by the advertisement written by a man named Mike who recommended going up the western coast of Iceland to the northernmost area full of fjords and cliffs where thousands of puffins spent their summers.

The end result of all this Googling and cogitation was my July week spent in Iceland. My guide was not only thoroughly informed about birds but about geology, having studied the subject in his college days. The drive from Rykjavik to Landsjbarg took the better part of a day, and we saw amazing evidence of volcanic activity such as mountains of skree that Mike told me were virtually unscalable because the tiny rock and ash particles allow for no footholds to be established. Only the famed Iceland sheep can maneuver the slopes, a fact that delighted me because it meant no bands of climbers making inroads into the natural environment. Those sheep became a lagniappe for me on my pilgrimage to see the puffins. Because there were so many of them feeding in fields with no human dwellings visible for miles and miles, I assumed them to be feral, some truly "wild" part of the landscape, introduced by humans, surely, but long since left to fend for themselves. I should have known better, since on the days I had been in the capital, I'd passed numerous shops displaying elegant woolen items in windows. Of course, my patient guide assured me that the sheep have shepherds who round them up periodically for shearing.

He also told me that Iceland does not want to join the

European Union because they would be forced to send some of their sheep to other countries and, more seriously, to accept into their herds sheep from elsewhere. They are sure their animals are superior even to Australian varieties and so wish to protect them from cross-breeding.

All morning, once we were outside the extended boundaries of the capital, we met no other vehicle and saw no other human beings. Lots of the distinctly squat sheep, a few indigenous ponies, and even fewer rooftops down by the sea that Mike said were part of isolated farms—these were what we drove past, allowing me to register that this was my first experience of being in what ecologists would term "wilderness." It felt entirely familiar at some deep emotional level, and I thought of Desert Fathers or other hermitic pilgrims who sought such environs in order to contemplate without interruption their own souls' relationship to some higher power or "god." And this trip certainly was a pilgrimage, since I had read about puffins before leaving, knew I wanted to sit alone at dawn and watch for the little sea birds to exit their deep cliff-edge burrows, and had thought quite a bit about my passionate attachment to these creatures.

The ontological question for me is, "Why puffins, of all the possible birds to choose as a talismanic focus?" If I wanted color, why didn't I gravitate toward parrots or tucans. If I wanted to help bring back endangered species, why not support efforts on behalf of peregrine falcons or pileated woodpeckers? And, if I preferred reclusive birds, why not fixate on owls? What is it about puffins?

My research into the composition and habits of my iconic birds may shed light on this riddle. Their genus name is Fratercula, coming from Latin and meaning "little brother." So their marked black and white plumage must have reminded early observers of monastic robes. The English name for them, "puffin," is Anglo-Norman or Middle English (*pophyn* and *poffin*), referring to the cured carcasses of nestling Manx Shearwater, another shore bird whose name comes from their common habitat's being the coasts of Great Britain and Ireland, near the Isle of Man. The puffin's closest ornithological relatives are auks, somewhat larger, much less colorful, but having similar behaviors. Within the genus are at least three sub-groups—tufted puffins, horned puffins, and, most recently, Atlantic puffins. The summer habitat for tufted and horned varieties is the North

Pacific region including British Columbia, Alaska, Siberia, and the Aleutians. These two groups winter in California, the Baja Peninsula, and Honshu, in Japan. The Atlantic puffin obviously summers in the Northern Atlantic beginning in Maine and going all the way to Iceland.

My puffins, the Atlantic variety, mate for life unless strange climatic conditions cause one or the other to wind up dead or part of a new colony. The male birds build the nests, which are burrows that may tunnel up to nine feet into the soft soil at the top of cliff faces. Couples try very hard to return year after year to their same burrows. These burrows are carefully lined with grass, leaves, and feathers, and the eggs laid and brooded therein are an off-white that occasionally has lilac tinges. Only one egg is laid each summer, and both parents incubate and feed it, taking turns flying out to sea to garner the little silver fishes for their baby to eat. The parent left inside the burrow gathers the lone and crucial egg against its brood patch with its wings, warming the tiny life inside as it develops. Once fledged, pufflings spend about five years at sea before they return to the colony site of their birth and find a mate of their own. Once the breeding season ends—usually by mid-August—all puffin species winter far out at sea. Because they inhabit both the sky and the water, they accomplish this feat by beating their stubby wings to cover miles and then diving into the sea for small fishes to give them much-needed energy and sustenance.

Physically, puffins are not especially impressive. They are stocky birds with very short wings and tails, black on their external parts and white or brownish-grey on their under parts. Their heads are capped in absolute black while their faces are white. Orange feet coordinate with their famous bills that are orange and red and black during breeding season. These bills fall off after their babies fledge, leaving them with a more muted coloration on their bills for the rest of their year at sea. At their most colorful stage, the bills have a narrow orange-red streak down the middle. Immediately next to this center stripe is a border that is pinkish beige, setting off the more primary tinge. Then there is a patch of mottled grey, again on either side, underlying the symmetry of this prominent proboscis. Finally, perpendicular to the bill itself are two small hooks of dark yellow or maize, offsetting the bill and causing it to stand out even more than it would without these facial accent marks.

None of the sources I consulted reported an obvious truth I confirmed with my guide—males and females are colored exactly the same and are not appreciably different in size. That means when a human being sees a puffin, s/he does not know whether it is male or female. Obviously, this "sameness" does not confuse the puffins, since they have no trouble reproducing themselves through heterosexual coupling, nor do they mistake their mate from the vast colony of identically marked birds.

What struck me about this anomaly is how different it is from human gender marking. In the 1970s, when some men began letting their hair grow quite long, I remember hearing little children ask a parent, "Is that a boy or a girl?" referring to a person walking with another person in front of them on the sidewalk. Why was it so important to that very young person to know what gender someone else occupied? Well, in the natural order of things, in the case of the Fratercula, we humans will just have to keep wondering since there are no visible clues to ease our anxiety over this particular taxonomy.

Another significant facet of their behavior in my estimation is this: while puffins are quite vocal during breeding and brooding season, they are silent at sea as they fly quite high above the water below them, usually about thirty feet, compared with their auk cousins who fly only five feet above the sea. And, finally, puffins by some name or other, are quite ancient. Fossils found in Oregon date as far back as the Late Miocene period (23.0-5.3 million years ago). North Carolina fossils may extend to the early Pliocene period (5.3-2.5 million years ago).

Most descriptions of puffins do not speak about their eyes, yet it is those eyes that stand out to me, especially now that I've been within four feet of the actual little birds. Tiny and round, they are set tightly into the slick white cheeks surrounding them. All the white makes their red cast stand out so they sear their way into your consciousness if you look directly at them, even in a static photograph. As I crouched nearby the four Icelandic puffins who graced me by not flying away in my presence, it was their eyes that held me. I felt as if I were being invited into a world outside my limited human scope, into a silent but powerful universe where I could comprehend without needing to know particulars and where I could feel like just one of many species of beings held in the balance of a power far greater than any of us. In other words, I felt as I had years before standing behind Niagara Falls in Canada and as I had recently as I watched tens of thousands of wildebeests crossing my horizon line as they migrated to greener feeding grounds with their young scampering behind them. I felt in the presence of the God of my understanding, never mind that the current manifestation was a small black and white bird unafraid to perch so near me.

One of the visiting rectors of my church said in a sermon recently that we should try to achieve what he called "a radical detachment from distractions so we can prefer nothing to the love of Christ." These days I often work to have a clear sense of what Christ's love means to me. Surely it involves submitting my selfish hopes and desires to a larger plan or purpose; surely it involves acceptance of those who lie outside my narrow experiences of life; surely it directs me to love of the sort C.S. Lewis termed "agape," a generalized caring for one's fellow human beings, quite distinct from erotic love for a particular individual. Agape love does not depend on rank or agreement about politics or skin color. These quality as those "distractions" enumerated in the visiting priest's sermon; they draw me away from the simple but arduous outlines for daily living found in Jesus' own dealings with those he met and served.

So, as I surrendered to sitting atop the cliffs at Landjsburg waiting for a sleepy puffin to step outside her or his burrow, and later, to holding myself as still as I know how to do, just feet from the four generous puffins who let me get close to them, I knew what the preacher had meant. All distractions had fallen away during those two hours, just as they do when I am in my garden in Minneapolis or when I listen to the choir at the Basilica sing certain pieces. In that dawn in Iceland, then, I was left open to the wonder of the little birds with colorful faces and piercing eyes, open to their ability to connect me to my deepest spiritual self. And, as I crouched before the puffin who made direct eye contact with me, I felt very clear about loving as Christ directs me. So my suspended moments at the cliff were more than a pantheistic experience. Rather than feeling awe-inspired, I found myself praying for the capacity to take in more faces that present themselves to me every day in my neighborhood or in less familiar places like airports or department stores. In a word, I want to register or take in or "see" more of the ordinary human beings who comprise my daily life. Rabbi Heschel once said to a man who worried that his "good" deeds were not pure enough, since he undertook them in order to feel better about himself rather than out of some purely generous motive, "The act teaches you the meaning of the act." It was my willingness to sit in the cold early morning light that taught me why I was doing that—so I could witness God's creation more intimately and fully. As I was recording my morning in my diary the next evening, I knew that time with the puffins now belongs in the same spiritual world as standing behind Niagara Falls, walking in the dawn-light of Assisi, absorbing the scope and depth of Tanzania, digging in the soil of my backyard, and truly seeing other human beings in all their stunning complexities.

Coda

In her famous poem, "Diving into the Wreck," Adrienne Rich likens a woman's need to delve into her psyche to discover who she really is to Jacque Cousteau's dives into the ocean depths. In his poem, "Digging," Seamus Heaney asserts that he will "dig" with his pen as he writes, just as his father digs with a spade to cut turf. Both these poets understand something I have been doing in this memoir as I have pushed myself further into anatomizing my current understanding of God and the path I have traveled to arrive where I am now. At the outset, I spoke of my bad habit of not digging deep enough holes to plant fall bulbs so as to insure healthy blooms in the spring and of how, on more complicated levels, I have also stopped short of my own digging or diving. Well, these pages represent a new effort to push further and see more clearly. The results seem to me a genuine paradox, hence something I cannot hope to resolve or answer or settle, since it is in the very nature of paradoxes to defy any such endings.

What I've found instead is a strange but powerful juxtaposition of my wanting to worship according to traditional and in some senses conservative formats even as I have come to comprehend God as defying definitions that usually accompany such practices. Similarly, I have become ever surer that the God of my understanding loves me not in spite of my being a lesbian or a feminist or a radical Democrat but because I occupy those states of being. Additionally, I now affirm that I want to practice my spiritual life in concert with others, even if some of them are not as encompassing in their ideas of what constitutes a "believer" as I and my higher power are.

In the middle of writing this spiritual memoir, I broke my right ankle on a Sunday morning when life seemed particularly good to me. I'd been to church where we'd been graced by one of our visiting celebrants who had delivered a stirring homily about ways to put Christ's idea of love into practice in today's strained and rapid world. In an instant my whole life changed, leaving me lying virtually all day and night either on my living room sofa or the narrow hospital bed installed in the first floor sunroom since I couldn't manage stairs in my cast. The first two and a half months of recovery taught me two invaluable spiritual lessons: patience with a process that simply couldn't be rushed, and acceptance that many people loved me and actually wanted to do things to ease my path back to myself. Various friends remarked after visiting me that I was not angry over having my life interrupted so violently. It never occurred to me to be angry, though I registered that once I might well have been furious. I felt sure that the God of my understanding wouldn't have let me experience a classic accident unless there were lessons for me to learn. Concentrating on recovery changed me, so that when I returned to this memoir, I understood that the meta-narrative contained in it swirled around a series of fundamental paradoxes. Being physically injured caused me to sharpen some of my spiritual muscles. Lying still most of the time freed my mind to consider what it meant that so many people volunteered to bring me delicious food, run errands for me, take me out for lovely rides around the lakes of my home town. Learning to ask for help made me feel strong and sure of myself rather than dependent or weak.

These small paradoxes seem now to dovetail into the paradox at the very heart of my current spiritual life. Because I've embraced something unresolvable, I no longer worry over what may seem strange contradictions to many of my friends because I affiliate with a church whose formal tenets frankly appall me. Rather I just continue being comfortable with the God I have carved out for myself, and committed to living a life that echoes many of the tenets laid down by Jesus during his time on earth.

Pursuing the writing of this spiritual memoir has done at least two central things: it has let me accept the inherent paradox arising from my preference for conservative spiritual practices while remaining clear-eyed about my radical politics; and it has opened new avenues for me to pursue as I continue to strengthen my commitment to "doing good." Sometimes it seems that my earliest introduction to God on those Saturdays when I accompanied my mother to our little Episcopal church and played among the pews laid the foundation for my current understanding of my faith. Belief need not harden into inflexible creeds or harsh judgments of other people's way of finding meaning; rather it can enliven our lives and keep us open to wonder and joy in God's amazing creation in all its diversity. So I will move into my future doing as Henry James recommended as the only way to manage life in a complex world—I will "hang fire," not insisting on consistency or certainty or even agreement.

About the Author

Toni McNaron is an educator, memoirist and lesbian feminist critic who taught literature and Women's Studies at the University of Minnesota for 37 years before retiring as a Distinguished Teaching Professor.

She is the author of a previous memoir, *I Dwell in Possibility*; and an ethnographic study of homophobia in the academy, *Poisoned Ivy: Lesbian and Gay Academics Confront Homophobia*. She has edited *The Sister Bond: A Feminist View of a Timeless Connection* and co-edited *Voices in the Night: Women Speaking About Incest* and *New Lesbian Studies: Into the 21st Century*.

While at the University of Minnesota (1964-2001), she began and chaired the Women's Studies Program, the Center for Advanced Feminist Studies, and the GLBT Studies Program.

Her current writing project is a collection of essays entitled *An Amethyst Remembrance*, written over four decades.

Made in the USA
Charleston, SC
15 November 2013